WE'LL DANCE WHEN THE GHOST WALKS

BY ANNETTE-FRANCES B

i

ISBN 978-1-7398885-3-4

Published in the UK by:

Louannvee Publishing
www.louannveepublishing.co.uk

To Les Cygne Four – Louis (my father),

Ida, Dora and Jack

and

To Vera (my mother)

With thanks to all family members for sharing their tales and allowing me to write them.

A big thank you to my husband, sons, daughters-in-law and grandchildren for their encouragement with this project.

NEWSPAPER SNIPPETS

"Les Cygne Four gave an exciting demonstration of the kind of dancing in which the ladies are thrown about in a way that suggests that at any moment one of them will come flying into the audience, but they remained cheerful and unruffled through it." 20th August 1940, p.3

"…brilliant dancing act by Les Cygne Four." (Blackpool)

"Les Cygne Four are expert dancers." (Glasgow)

"Les Cygne Four have several excellent dances in which originality of treatment is abetted by capital timing, and talent in various directions…" (Brixton)

"…admirable dancing from Les Cygne Four." (Liverpool)

"The Les Cygne Four give one of the finest acts of adagio dancing seen for a long while…" (Swindon)

"Favourites are Les Cygne Four adagio dancers, who are graceful and thrilling." (Southampton)

"There is plenty to admire, too, in the agile and distinctive adagio dancing of Les Cygne Four, who are certainly expert in this type of entertainment…" (London)

CONTENTS
PART ONE
BACKGROUND SNIPPETS – FROM 1917

PART TWO
TREADING THE BOARDS – FROM 1932

PART ONE
BACKGROUND SNIPPETS
FROM 1917

Family characters – main characters in bold

William Bernard W. – b. 1871 m. Annie Louisa –
b. 19th August 1878
Hilda – b. 5th June 1897
Dora – b. 22nd December 1898
Madeleine – b. 26th September 1907
Ida – b. 22nd January 1909
Louis – b. 6th June 1911
Joan – b. June 1919
Jack C.D.L. – b. 7th May 1901 (married Dora)

CHAPTER 1
FAMILY LIFE

The Webb family lived near Handsworth in Birmingham
(UK). Their home comprised a large Victorian, semi-
detached affair, spread over four floors, including a large
cellar. With the exception of the front parlour, which
was kept for entertaining visitors, every room was well
used. The perfect home for a large, lively family with
many interests and much energy to expend.

Annie Louisa Webb (Mother or Mama) was a strong-
minded, well organised, musical being. A mere five-foot-
one, with her shoes on, she no longer possessed a slim,
neat body for giving birth to so many children had rather
extended her figure, but the combination of Welsh and

French ancestry had certainly added character and perhaps a little beauty to her face.

William Bernard Webb (Father or Papa) a senior toolmaker by trade, was a sensible, industrious man, in his early forties, content with his position in a factory, originally owned by his father and uncle, but now owned by his cousin. His flaxen hair and bright blue eyes contrasted favourably with Annie Louisa's somewhat dramatic looks. Like his wife, William was also quite small – a mere five-foot-four and a half inches, but his character was strong. As an avid amateur historian, keen reader, cyclist and chess player, William's time was never wasted. In temperament he was rather like a well-trained lion, quietly contented when all was well with his world, his slippers warming by the fire and food waiting for him, but quick to launch an attack, with an angry growl, when people or situations failed him.

Both parents expected high standards from all their children. Father encouraged their best at all times. Mama demanded their constant self-improvement, both academically and morally and had been known to impose drastic penalties upon any miniature individuals who dared to oppose her.

Little Louis, at the tender age of six, was once sent to his room, supposedly for a whole day, with no daytime clothes, no toys and only one book to read, because he ventured to defy his mama, by protesting when told to get ready for church.

Stamping his foot, he shouted: 'But our mama, it's no fun and it's always cold. I want to stay home and play.'

Looking sternly down at her rebellious son, Mama quietly replied: 'Very well, you shall stay in your room, with no day clothes and with no toys. You shall read your book of saints. Papa went to the early Mass so he'll be home and will see that you fulfil my wishes.'

Being rather a determined little boy, Louis remained in his room, ignoring the book, instead playing make believe games, pretending he was travelling on a boat to faraway lands, encountering and fighting with pirates. His imagination knew no boundaries.

Eventually the rest of the family returned home from church, the younger three girls giggling and chattering happily as they clattered up the stairs to their room, whilst Hilda and Dora, the two elder girls, remained downstairs helping their mother prepare some tea and cakes.

Louis waited until he heard several taps on the front door, followed swiftly by the slightly chaotic cacophony of female chatter intermingled with the clatter of china cups and saucers. Silently he crept downstairs, wrapped only in his underwear and an eiderdown, and peered into the large front parlour, where his mother was now entertaining her church lady friends, with tea and cakes. To his mother's horror, all faces turned suddenly, towards the pathetic little figure of a sparsely dressed tiny boy, quite short and skinny for his age, uttering an *apparently timid* and pitiful:

'I'm sorry, Mama, I won't be bad again. Please, please could I have a drink and, and some food now? I'm sooo hungry.'

Despite his mother's assurance that Louis had *needed* to be in his room, because of his bad behaviour and that he *had* been given breakfast and plenty to drink, an army of well meaning, motherly church women plied the *poor little tot* with numerous delicious cakes and cups of milk. Eventually the benevolent church ladies slowly dispersed, to their respective homes and families, possibly thinking that Annie's children were often kept half starved, in cold attics with no clothes and forbidden any home comforts!

In spite of a somewhat strict way of life, the children always ran to their parents with any tears and troubles, for they knew they would be understood and comforted. They felt secure.

Music played an important part in family life, for in the dim, distant days before television, families generally tended to make their own entertainment. All William and Annie's children were encouraged to play an instrument, sing and even to dance a little. There were two pianos, one in the living room for practice and one in the front parlour for guests to use or listen to.

Hilda, the eldest girl, enjoyed music, but preferred to sit doing needlework and watch whilst the younger children performed. She acted as a second mother to the large, ever-growing family, bathing and caring for them whenever her mother was busy. Hilda was in demand a great deal on Tuesdays and Wednesdays, for on those days her mother was needed in the little corner shop that she leased and supervised. A lady was employed to help the family with some of the washing and ironing, but Hilda would prepare a meal and care for the younger children.

Dora, just a year younger than Hilda and the total opposite in character, lacked any streak of domesticity. Her whole life was a wonderful whirl of music and dance. She played the piano well, though after a while would become bored simply sitting and would spring up and dance energetically around the living room, while Madeleine, one of the younger children, would take over on the piano.

Dora was deemed the prettiest of the girls, her shoulder length, wavy hair shone with a natural flaxen glow. Her eyes were bright blue, beautifully expressive and edged with luscious, long brown lashes, further complemented by dark eyebrows.

Madeleine, quite a few years younger than Dora and Hilda, was a tiny, merry little child with long, wavy dark hair, brown eyes and a clever, mischievous nature. Next came Ida and then Louis, the only surviving boy. Joan, the baby of the family, was generally loved and fussed over by everyone as she mimicked their actions, with the natural comical antics that only a toddler could perfect.

Ida was the tomboy of the family. Her doll would be ignored in favour of a game of whip and top, marbles, conkers or daring, outdoor adventures with brother Louis and his friends, many of whom were much older than him. Louis didn't mind Ida tagging along, indeed he rather enjoyed showing off and teasing her a little, but she was a tough little thing, determined to be *one of the gang* and needless to say Louis' lively antics led Ida into many a drastic situation. One particular incident, however, ensured Ida of high status and everlasting admiration amidst Louis' friends. Louis and his best friend Tommy had developed a sudden and passionate craze on boxing, in the little lane at the back of the house, and to Ida's absolute indignation, both boys refused to let her take a turn...

'No, you're far too weak, silly, you're a girl,' scorned Tommy.

'He's right,' agreed Louis. 'Mama would never forgive me if you were to be hurt.'

'Oh please, go on, our Louis, let me just borrow them

for a little while,' pleaded Ida with a flicker of her pretty eyelashes. 'I won't tell Mama,' Ida persisted in a persuasive tone.

'Oh go on then,' said Louis flinging his boxing gloves on the ground. 'You'll be sorry though, it's bound to end in tears.'

Ida pushed her bouncy fair hair firmly behind her ears and picked up the boxing gloves, grinning in delight. Her blue eyes glistened brightly with excitement.

Soon a little circle of boys gathered around in interest, as Ida pushed her slender hands into the firm leather and horse-hair boxing gloves and bounced energetically from side to side, elbows bent, gloved hands at shoulder level, punching the air. 'Who dares box with me?' There was silence.

'Best pick someone little, because you're not as strong as us, you're just a girl,' advised Louis.

'I'm brainier and stronger than the lot of you and more than a year older than you, our Louis,' retorted Ida. 'Come on, Tommy, I dare you.'

'But he's much bigger than you,' protested Louis.

'I'll tell our mama you let me wear the boxing gloves…'

'You're going to have to box her, Tommy,' decided Louis.

'I'm not boxing a girl,' retorted Tommy.

'She'll tell my mama we let her use the gloves if you don't and you'll be for it as well I expect.'

Ultimately, to the delight of an ever-expanding circle of boys all keen to observe and possibly laugh at the results of Ida's determination, it was finally decided that the match should proceed, with no allowances made for Ida's somewhat petite feminine frame.

'Now wait until our Louis has counted to three and then the match will begin,' demanded Ida with an air of absolute authority.

Louis dutifully counted to three and before anyone had time to blink, Ida dealt Tommy a firm, fierce blow upon his chin and poor Tommy was stretched flat on his back, in the mud, with a horrible, surprised expression upon his face. Ida had knocked him unconscious!

'Oh, our Ida,' scolded Louis, with a mixture of horror and admiration. 'You've knocked him cold, quick, run tell our mama!'

Luckily Tommy was only mildly concussed and soon recovered, though he didn't quite have the same enjoyment for boxing after that. Needless to say, Ida and Louis were severely reprimanded and the following January Ida's birthday plea for boxing gloves went unheeded.

CHAPTER 2
YOUNG ENTERTAINERS

As the children grew a little older, their interest in drama, music and dance grew stronger. Their mother encouraged them to create their own little concerts and perform in the front parlour, for special friends and family members. She often participated in the entertainment, singing solo in her beautiful soprano voice. Father helped to create simple scenery and props.

These little concerts were perhaps their way of coping with life's harder times. They helped to unite the family and maybe take their minds away from tragedy, troubles and loss. For the family *had* experienced much tragedy. Whilst six children remained happy and healthy, three brothers had sadly died. Harold, a bright, caring child, lived to ten and then succumbed to peritonitis. Edward, a flaxen haired boy with beautiful blue eyes, lived to just six. He died in a tragic accident at home, whilst in the care of a paid nursemaid. The nursemaid was covering for Annie, while she visited Hilda in hospital. For many years Hilda blamed herself for being the cause of her mother's absence from the house. Another son, Bernard, was born with pneumonia and survived only a short while.

Despite this loss, or perhaps because of it, the family were fiercely protective of one another, determined to keep busy, determined to hone their creative skills and to share them with others.

One year, just before Christmas, William gathered the family in the living room for a special family meeting. He looked a little apprehensive as he waited for them to seat themselves. 'Rather bad news I'm afraid. The firm's

Christmas Concert Party's cancelled. The entertainers are ill, some sort of nasty sickness I believe. I'm so sorry, I know how much you all enjoy going. But all is not lost, because…' William paused, took a deep breath and continued, 'because, it's, well it's been suggested, by your mama and agreed by Cousin Paul, that we perform our own little family concert. We'd really be helping and…' William's voice was drowned in an avalanche of loud squeals of excitement from the younger children and animated questions from Hilda and Dora.

William sat down silently in his armchair, momentarily out of his depth amidst so much chaotic chatter. Soon, regaining confidence and dignity, he stood, raising himself to his full five-foot-four and a half inches and roared: 'Silence!'

Instantly the uproar ceased, family members sat, devoid of all movement and sound.

'NOW, let me finish,' he demanded. 'If we *do* take up this responsibility it will mean much hard work, you'll need to practise each evening, because we've only two weeks to plan, prepare and perfect a concert fit to be seen by all the factory and office workers and their families. You will all need to design and create outfits as well. Our Hilda, could your fiancé spare you to help supervise the needlework?' Hilda, in her mid-twenties, was engaged to a successful businessman, a widower considerably her senior in age, but nevertheless charming and still quite attractive.

Hilda nodded. 'I'll rummage through the spare material box and see what I can find to start us off.' As a skilled dressmaker and tailoress, Hilda already made many of the children's clothes and took a few private orders from local families as well. Her talents would be invaluable.

Annie rose from her chair and stood beside her husband. 'All adults and children in agreement with creating and performing in a family concert, raise your right hand,' she called. All hands rose. Unable to successfully differentiate between *right* and *left*, little Joan raised both.

'Very well,' said William, 'that's settled; we're all in agreement. The employees and their families will be really happy. Paul said that a small amount will be paid to us, just to cover any expenses we may have. We can vote whether to keep it or not or whether to donate it to a good cause, when we have a clearer understanding of our expenses.'

For almost two whole weeks life was dominated by a wave of dedicated planning, preparation and rehearsal for the forthcoming concert party. At one point, the atmosphere was saturated in a surprising silence, as everyone focused diligently upon the task of decorating Hilda's carefully made costumes, with a range of fancy buttons, ribbons and colourful patches – even little Joan, sat on Hilda's knee carefully helping to sew new ribbons onto her ballet shoes.

Occasionally the silence was interspersed with the gentle hum of quiet, almost clandestine conversation, as several apparently major democratic decisions were made regarding the range of songs, dances and short comical sketches to be offered and by whom. This strangely organised and peaceful aura was sporadically punctuated by wild, over-enthusiastic sessions of rehearsal, frequently ending in either tears or laughter.

Gradually the hours and days of dedication proved fruitful, and the family were ready to discuss and plan a basic, one page programme. Mother wrote the programme and Madeleine carefully decorated the edges with a series of elegant patterns, mainly comprising flowers, simple shapes and music notes, using her best ink pen. Hilda's fiancé kindly offered to pay for a number of copies to be printed. There was great excitement when he arrived at the house, early one evening, carrying a brown package containing the freshly printed programmes.

Gingerly, Mother opened the package, taking care not to damage the precious and much awaited contents. She took out one programme and allowed each child and adult to inspect it. 'Now,' she said, 'this one is ours, but the rest must remain within the package and none of you are to touch them. Is that understood?'

Everyone nodded gravely.

'Mama, our names are all on those programmes, shall we be famous now?' asked young Louis, half joking, half serious.

'Not yet,' replied his mother smiling. 'But perhaps one day, if you work hard at school your name may be known by many. You know you can achieve almost anything if you work hard.'

CHAPTER 3
AND SO, IT BEGINS

The family concert party was scheduled to be performed on a Saturday afternoon and again in the early evening. As the time drew nearer family rehearsals increased in quantity, the atmosphere became tense, and tears and tantrums were abundant as each child and adult aimed for perfection.

William arrived home from work earlier than usual one evening, just in time to witness woeful wailing from little Joan in floods of tears because she'd forgotten her dance steps; Dora becoming frustrated with young Madeleine as she played an incorrect note on the piano; Louis and Ida arguing fiercely about who should tidy their simple props away and Hilda, hands on hips, raising her voice above the din in an effort to maintain order whilst awaiting Mama's return from her little shop.

William walked into the living room, still in his outdoor shoes and still carrying his large black umbrella. 'Silence… enough,' he roared as he proceeded to bang the steel end of his umbrella unceremoniously, in fact quite viciously, upon the wooden floor, to gain their full attention. 'This behaviour is not becoming. Hilda and Dora, you are young ladies now, please set an example to your younger sisters and brother. The concert party's in four days. There will be no more rehearsals until the day before the event.'

'But, but… Papa, Papa…' said Joan, gulping desperately for enough breath to speak between her tears. 'I like dancing. Am I not allowed to dance?' William felt emotions threatening to overwhelm him, as he witnessed little Joan's sorrowful state. His response was swift and kind. 'You shall dance whenever you like, for your own pleasure, but we shall not practise for the show, as a family, until this Friday – the day before the show.' He patted little Joan gently on the head before continuing, 'You've all overstretched yourselves. It's important you all do your best and I know you will, but it's also important to *enjoy* performing. If you're happy and confident the audience will be happy and have confidence in you. Now, you all need a rest.'

William's decision regarding a total break from rehearsals proved prudent. The family seemed to gain confidence. They were revitalised and carried out their final rehearsal, on the Friday evening, minus any tears or tantrums. There were several minor mistakes, but they coped with them calmly.

The next day, Saturday, the family were united in their efforts to perform to perfection. The large hall, allocated for the concert party, echoed horribly, the floor was extremely uneven and awkward for the girls to dance on, little Joan tripped twice, but bravely soldiered on and was greeted with enthusiastic applause. Swiftly and confidently, she smiled before running over to hug her mother.

A previously requested small table, promised to Louis and Ida for a comical kitchen scene, was totally overlooked. Undefeated they spread their tablecloth on the dusty floor, placed their cups and saucers upon it, sat on the floor and proceeded to make the audience laugh as they performed their hilarious sketch, written for them by Hilda's fiancé, John.

Next came their mother's solo. Her chosen songs were well received. Thankfully the piano provided was in tune and Madeleine was able to play it with confidence and competence. Dora also played a beautiful piece and later performed a delightful dance, accompanied by her younger sisters.

Just prior to the finale, little Joan walked slowly towards the eager onlookers, cuddling and rocking a baby doll in her arms, gazing tenderly at her *baby* as she sang a gentle lullaby. The audience of typists, clerks, directors, factory workers, their children and senior family members were mesmerised and quite moved. Several – including a retired army officer – reached discreetly for their cotton handkerchiefs. For the finale the whole family, including Hilda and Father, appeared together to sing a lively Christmas song and to thank their audience. Everyone applauded with gusto. It appeared the family concert party was considered a success.

Courtesy of a small, ultimately bi-annual feature in the local newspaper, word quickly spread and soon they were receiving requests from other large firms, local schools and some charitable organisations, asking them to entertain at various functions. This was to be the beginning of a family pastime that lasted for a number of years, evolving to meet the needs of their audience and to accommodate the skills and creative interests of the younger family members as they travelled towards teenage years, work and adulthood.

William helped 'behind the scenes', with props and scenery. Annie was responsible for hiring the various halls, accepting bookings, dealing with finance and generally organising everyone. She also sang solo and as part of a duet, depending on the theme of the concert party.

Dora and Ida danced and performed comical

sketches. Joan did cute little numbers, singing and dancing. Louis performed humorous sketches with Ida and various family members. Madeleine did mostly singing and piano playing, with a little dancing and occasional comedy sketches with Louis. A small fee was charged for each performance and generally they managed to cover all their expenses. Any money left over was *kept for a rainy day...*

Left – Louis, age 15 as Buttons in a pantomime
Right – Louis, age 15 in a family concert party
Reproduced with the permission of the
Library of Birmingham.
From the Ernest Dyche Collection

CHAPTER 4
KINDRED SPIRITS

Within months of that first concert party, Hilda married her fiancé, John, and was rapidly whisked across the sea to live in his family home in Ireland. Originally sent to Birmingham for two years, to help establish a new branch, John's mission was now accomplished and the main branch, in Ireland, was pining for his skills once more. Hilda was sadly missed by everyone, not least for her motherly ways and her wonderful skills with cooking and needlework. Dora and younger sister Ida became responsible for designing and creating the costumes, aided by ideas from Madeleine, Louis and little Joan.

Deprived of Hilda's caring presence, the family were soon to be partially compensated for her absence, or at least *distracted* by Jack, her adult stepson. Having finished his time at Dublin University, Jack had secured a position in the same firm as his father, but as part of his training, was to be sent to the London branch for a few weeks and then onto the Birmingham branch for two years, hence William and Annie were asked if they could *keep an eye* on him.

Once safely installed in rooms in Birmingham, Jack firmly established himself as a member of the family, visiting them every evening and at weekends. In fact, Jack burst into their lives, transforming them forever! Initially the girls thought he looked extremely handsome, but rather dull. Ultimately, however, they discovered that appearances can be deceptive. By day Jack worked quietly within a busy office, dressed in a smart suit and carrying his black umbrella and briefcase, but each evening he flew swiftly and energetically into their living room and proceeded to elicit lively laughter as he recalled, with his soft Irish accent and in dramatic fashion, various people and situations he had encountered throughout his day, whilst travelling to and from work. As a talented artist, he carried a pencil and sketch book with him at all times and was often able to show the family comical drawings to accompany his tales.

Jack took a keen interest in the family concert parties and was soon volunteering to write some new humorous sketches for them to perform. His fine baritone voice was also put to good use, in the form of a duet with Annie and some solo pieces.

Having been taught Irish dance, by his elder sister, Jack was never happier than when moving to music. He longed to dance all day, every day. As an avid theatregoer, he was totally entranced by the rhythm, speed and skill of tap dance. He was, in fact, totally stage struck and yearned one day to walk away from his humdrum office job and venture into the real theatre to earn his living.

Knowing that Annie's younger girls attended dance lessons, occasionally accompanied by young Louis, one evening Jack asked her if she would like him to walk down to meet them.

'That's kind of you, Jack,' she said smiling. 'I do worry about them walking back on these darker autumn evenings.'

With a set of hurried verbal directions from Annie, Jack set out eagerly to meet them. The streets were barely visible in the semi-darkness. Inadvertently he took a wrong turning, entered and startled a group of elderly women who were sitting drinking tea and crocheting.

'My sincere apologies, ladies, I'm looking for a dance school,' said Jack, with a slight bow and a swift smile.

At the sight of such a dashing young man, one extremely wrinkled lady, rather frail in appearance, threw down her crochet, leapt to her feet, marched rapidly towards Jack and took both his firm, young hands within her thin, bony fingers. 'I'll teach you to dance, young sir,' she uttered, with a smile revealing a row of black, chipped front teeth.

'Thank you. That would be lovely another day perhaps,' replied Jack, as he extricated himself from the lady's grasp and backed away rapidly. Once at a safe distance he paused, gave another little bow and then positively ran back through the outer door.

Back in the street and at a safe distance from the room of elderly ladies, Jack stopped for a moment, to recall Annie's original directions, realised his mistake and proceeded to take the correct route to the ballet school, running all the way at full speed, ultimately pushing wide the correct door and sinking swiftly onto a small wooden chair. He was dripping with perspiration and gasping for breath, as the heavy outer door crashed closed behind him.

A young lady playing a lively polka on a rather beaten-up old piano paused in surprise and fifteen little girls, approximately four to six in age, paused mid polka to stare directly at Jack. The young lady at the piano, stood and turned towards Jack, revealing her wonderful wavy, flaxen hair and sparkling blue eyes. In her early twenties, she was a perfect vision of beauty. To his horror, Jack recognised her, it was Dora.

'Whatever are you doing here, Jack?' she asked, looking at his somewhat dishevelled appearance. 'Is everyone alright at my home? Is there an emergency?' Dora sounded rather worried.

'N-n-no,' stammered an unusually flustered Jack. 'I came to meet the young ones from their lesson, but I went the wrong way and… well, I'll tell you about it later and sketch you some little pictures that will make you laugh,' he said, hurriedly regaining his usual poise and confidence. 'Where are your young sisters?'

Dora looked at Jack, an element of humour apparent in her vibrant blue eyes. 'Ida and Madeleine are in the class in the next room, but little Joan is here. Look, she's waving at you.'

Turning towards the row of previously dancing girls, Jack recognised little Joan giggling and waving at him. He waved back.

'Dora, I thought you were working late this evening. Why are you here this early and *why* are you playing the piano for children?' asked Jack.

'This is part of my work this evening,' replied Dora patiently. 'I did my normal dull day and then came here, to help Madame Lehmiski with the little ones and to play the piano for them, because her pianist had to go to a funeral. Then I've my adult dance lessons after. Now I wonder why you're *really* here, Jack.'

'That's grand to be playing for the little ones,' replied Jack. 'Well now, will you listen to my confession?'

Dora looked a little taken aback. 'Confession?'

'Yes, confession. Well perhaps I should just say my ulterior motive in offering to meet the young ones.' Jack hesitated for a moment, gathered his courage and then continued. 'Well, put simply, it's a discreet way of finding out about the adult tap lessons.'

Dora looked surprised. 'Why didn't you just ask me?

You knew I did adult dance.'

'Yes, but I needed to *see* the school, get the feel of the place and find out if any other males attend. I didn't want to be the only one.'

'That's no excuse, you still could have asked me,' said Dora smiling. 'If you wait a few moments, I'll introduce you to Madame Lehmiski, when the lesson ends. Madeleine, Ida and Joan will wait for you.'

Madame Lehmiski proved to be an interesting and highly intelligent, neat, slim, graceful lady. Dressed in a mid-calf length grey silk dress with small neat tassels around the hem and from the shoulders, a short string of small, pale blue beads and a long, narrow pale blue silk scarf, she drifted elegantly into view, smiled warmly at Jack and beckoned for him to sit opposite her, whilst Dora helped the children change from their ballet shoes and put on their outdoor clothing.

Instead of extolling the virtues of her dance school, Madame's first words to Jack were: 'Why would you like to learn to dance?' Followed quickly by: 'Have you ever danced before?'

'My sister taught me Irish dance, but I would like to learn tap,' replied Jack.

'To dance within our adult classes, it would benefit you to learn several disciplines of dance: including ballet and tap. You must be dedicated and hard-working. I do not teach adults, unless they work hard and show skill.'

Madame continued to emphasise the need for hard work and then requested that Jack audition before agreeing to teach him. Her manner was firm, but the bright sparkle in her eyes, combined with an intriguing and attractive little laugh indicated a good sense of humour.

Ultimately, it was established that Jack could attend the adult dance sessions with Dora each week and would begin within the intermediate group. Jack entered the world of dance with total commitment and absolute enthusiasm. His body, naturally elegant and well-coordinated, moved with spontaneity and rhythm, echoing the emotions of each musical piece.

Swiftly he was moved from Madame's intermediate to her advanced group. Swiftly he grasped the opportunity of asking Dora to partner him for several routines, suddenly realising as he did so that he was totally and utterly smitten by her beauty and her character. Strangely Jack had spent many hours in Dora's company each week, sharing meals, conversation, and family rehearsals amidst her lively, if slightly chaotic and sometimes vaguely unconventional family, yet he had remained blissfully unaware of Dora's growing influence upon his emotions. Now, suddenly, within the neutral atmosphere of the dance school, he was utterly aware of her influence, utterly aware of her magical spirit within his presence. *Whatever am I going to do,* thought Jack, *I think I love her...*

CHAPTER 5
QUEST FOR ADVENTURE

Jack and Dora's lives rapidly became explicably intertwined, as they shared dance lessons at Madame Lehmiski's. Their movements were exquisite as they partnered each other for several little routines. Soon Madame suggested they worked on a series of little dances and tap routines, to be included within some of her local productions. After work and at weekends their lives were pulsating with music and dance, as they rehearsed for Madame and for family concerts.

To Jack's delight, Dora's spirit was gradually drawn towards his as they chatted between rehearsals, sharing their dreams and plans for the future. Both were bored with their humdrum day jobs, both longed for excitement and adventure and both were deeply entranced and bewitched by the world of professional theatre. They began to plan a life together, a life free from monotonous predictability, a life together, as husband and wife touring the world as dancers.

One Saturday afternoon after a particularly busy family rehearsal, Jack approached William to ask for Dora's hand in marriage. William had escaped to the little breakfast room at the back of the house, as was his habit if his services were not required during family rehearsal. Jack knocked tentatively on the door.

'Come in,' called William, carefully replacing his china teacup in its saucer on the table beside him. 'Sit down. What can I do for you, young Jack?'

Jack sat nervously beside a warm coal fire, on a well-worn wooden chair. Facing William he clasped his hands together, holding them in front of his chest, as if in prayer. 'Please, please, sir, William, I love your daughter. I, I… we…'

The breakfast room door opened suddenly and Dora burst in. 'Father, Papa, we want to be married. I was supposed to wait outside, but…'

'Dora, this is unseemly behaviour. Please be calm. Now sit and wait for this young gentleman to complete his speech.'

'William, I love Dora and I humbly beseech your permission to marry her,' said Jack, his eyes glistening with emotion.

'Well, well, this is not entirely unexpected, but it still needs some careful consideration. Dora, bring in your mother please.'

Dora rapidly responded.

The four adults sat together in silence, broken finally by William. 'Now, Annie,' he said, addressing his wife. 'Young Jack and Dora want to be married.'

'Yes,' replied Annie, 'Dora's just told me.'

'Well, Annie. Jack is a good young man and has good prospects. What are your thoughts on the matter?'

'I like you, Jack,' said Annie, 'but, I think you should both get to know each other a little more before you commit to an engagement and marriage. Marriage is forever.' Annie paused for a moment. She appeared thoughtful. Eventually she continued, 'Also, Jack, our Hilda is married to your father which makes it all seem a little complicated; though there is no blood relationship between you.'

'But, Mother, Mama, we want to be married and tour the world tap dancing together. Jack's been writing to theatrical agents to find out what to do. We may have found a good agent. We just have to meet him.' Dora's voice was full of passion as she rose from her chair and stood before her mother, arms outstretched as if to encourage and grasp a positive reply. A sudden, ominous silence pervaded the room as William and Annie sat with looks of disbelief and horror upon their faces.

William was the first to speak: 'You're both excellent tap dancers and extremely talented young people, but it's strictly a pleasant pastime, a hobby. Jack, you cannot expect my daughter to join you in such a life. Your father would be shocked to think you were even planning such a thing.'

A seemingly impenetrable cloud of despair, so intense it was almost visible, descended upon the two young people as they walked slowly and silently from the room, Jack with his arm around Dora.

'Let's walk in the garden,' suggested Dora, 'it's easier to think outside.'

'Alright,' agreed Jack, somewhat despondently.

Now late afternoon, it was quite chilly, and the light was beginning to fade. After a rather brisk and silent walk around the garden, hand in hand, Dora whispered something into Jack's ear.

'Why are you whispering?' he asked.

'I, well, I don't really know, it just seemed to be necessary in case anyone was listening to us.'

'I'm not sure anyone in their right mind is out walking, in this frozen garden, at this hour. Most are a little more level-headed,' replied Jack. 'What was it you whispered?'

Dora repeated her words in normal speech form: 'I just said, we will not be defeated, nor will we defeat those who love us, our families.'

'Beautiful words,' agreed Jack. 'But, please explain. It

all seems so hopeless.'

Dora beckoned for Jack to sit beside her on a wooden garden chair. She spoke clearly and firmly: 'My family is worried about us. We're young and maybe a little wild, in their eyes. They don't understand, but they will if we work slowly. Carry on with our normal lives, court each other more openly and ensure they feel we're sensible and that we've given up our plans for the theatre. It may take a bit of time, but…'

'What about the agents. One was willing to see us?' asked Jack.

'Well… Perhaps we could sneak to see him and find out a little more, but during our normal working hours. Depending on where he's situated, I suppose,' replied Dora. 'But then take things slowly – if we can somehow…' Her eyes shone with a wild combination of love and excitement.

Jack was swift to catch her excitement and soon the pair were momentarily wrapped within each other's arms, before walking back into the warmth of Dora's family home.

Dora's suggested approach to her parents' apprehension seemed to work. She and Jack continued their normal work each day, threw themselves energetically into family and dance school rehearsals, but made no further mention of their plans to enter the theatre as professionals. Ultimately William and Annie were happy and delighted to welcome Jack *officially* into the family and in April 1922 Jack and Dora became husband and wife, amid much applause and family celebration – including a brief but happy reunion with Hilda and John.

Following the excitement of the wedding, life

returned to normality: church, family rehearsals, family shows, work for the adults and school for the children. Jack was granted permission to move into Dora's large front bedroom, which she had previously shared with Hilda. Ultimately of course it was hoped that they would find their own little house and raise a perfect family.

All was peaceful, all was normal or so it seemed, until quite unexpectedly one Monday morning the large front bedroom was strangely silent. The wardrobe door didn't open with its usual mild creak – it was already open, left swinging on its worn, brass hinges and had been for some time. There was no lively morning chatter or gentle laughter – silence reigned.

Young Ida knocked on the door. 'Are you two *still* sleeping? Jack will be late for work and I need my book. You had it last, Dora. I read it to you.'

Impatiently Ida went into the room. 'Please, Dora, I... Mama, Mama, they've gone... Their wardrobe's empty, they...'

Madeleine, Louis and little Joan joined Ida in the doorway of the uninhabited room. Joan started to cry and Madeleine hugged her.

'I think I know where they've gone,' exclaimed Louis, excitedly. 'To the theatre to tap dance for a living. I think I'm right.'

'Don't be silly, our Louis, they said they wouldn't. They're married now you know,' Madeleine replied with a playful, rather astute smile.

'What *is* all this commotion?' demanded Annie as she reached the top stair somewhat breathless.

'I was calling you. They've gone,' said Ida in dismay. 'Look.'

Rapidly and thoroughly Annie examined every

section of the room. 'There's an envelope here, addressed to *my family*. It's in our Dora's writing. Get yourselves neat and tidy for school and we'll read it together in the dining room.'

Neatly dressed and solemnly seated, Madeleine, Ida, Louis and little Joan listened with fierce concentration as their mother read the letter:

Dear Mama and Papa,

We have a wonderful opportunity to join a real theatrical show and tour England and Scotland tap dancing. It is too exciting to miss. We are catching the early morning train to London.

Please do not be cross with us or disappointed. We will not do anything that you would not approve of and if all goes wrong Jack can always do office work again, but I am certain he will not need to.

Please give the girls and Louis all our sincere wishes and love and tell them we will send them letters and visit as often as we can. If we do well, we will send money back to you, to help a little.

We remain your loving Dora and Jack.

CHAPTER 6
RETURN TO BASE

Whilst Jack and Dora began their initiation into the wonderful, unique, extremely tough world of show business, travelling around Britain, working hard and embracing each new experience, the rest of the family mourned their loss, with a rare mixture of anger and pride. Family concert parties continued, with roles changing slightly to cover for Dora and Jack's absence. Joan's dance spots increased in length and complexity as she grew a little older and her talent shone and now in their teenage years, Madeleine, Ida and Louis increased their input. Madeleine joined her mama to sing a duet, whilst Ida and Louis continued with their comedy sketches, Louis joined Madame Lehmiski's for regular dance lessons with his sisters and he and Ida added a dance routine to their repertoire. As time zigzagged along at a steady pace Louis, Ida and Madeleine joined the work force and considered themselves adults, albeit they were still very young teenagers. All had been offered the chance of continuing their studies, but all had felt the need to earn some money and help the family.

Madeleine, often called Madge by family and friends, worked in an office, for Jack's old firm in Birmingham – ultimately becoming one of the firm's directors and a shareholder. Ida did needlework by day and continued advanced dance studies and rehearsals most evenings. Louis took an apprenticeship in cabinet making. At fourteen he gave the impression of a quiet young man, with not too much to contribute to the average day-to-

day chitchat. He spent each day in a busy workshop sawing and shaping stubborn blocks of wood,
until they finally found their way into shops and exhibitions, in the form of wardrobes, bookcases and many other items of good quality furniture. Whilst still under apprenticeship, some afternoons were passed at a Birmingham school of art, improving his knowledge and skills at cabinet making and design. He stopped the adult dance lessons he'd been attending with Ida but remained an enthusiastic participant in family concert parties.

A few years later at nineteen – in 1930 – with a secure job and a reasonable salary, Louis felt trapped. A prisoner, to endless routine, he felt a desperate need to escape, for beneath his apparently introvert nature, was an extraordinary enthusiasm, an extraordinary desire for life's adventure. Realistically, he knew he should be grateful – whilst many people were unemployed and struggling to survive, he was able to pay his way and help his parents. Yet Louis' mind was captured in a whirl of fantastic dreams of excitement and adventure, possibly influenced by the many classic novels he read. He hoped, of course, to please his family, but felt a strong need for an element of originality and risk. He yearned to be presented with a real challenge, something that would give him the chance to prove himself as an individual.

Meanwhile – by 1930 – Jack and Dora had established an element of success as tap dancers and were generally to be found on tour, in digs, rehearsing or on stage throughout England, Ireland, Scotland and Wales. Every so often, however, they would re-join the family, filling the home with theatrical tales and laughter whilst informing Mama and Papa they were just resting between shows. Soon the whole family learned to associate *just resting* with actually being between bookings – not always a good place to be financially!

One chilly January afternoon, however, Madeleine arrived home from the office, just as Jack and Dora were approaching the front path. 'Well, this *is* a surprise,' she exclaimed as she hugged them both.

'We're home for Dora to rest, she's…' explained Jack.

'*I know*, you're between bookings – sorry, *just resting*,' replied Madeleine with a knowing smile.

'No, Dora's not *just resting* she needs *to rest*. She's suffering from total exhaustion.'

As if on cue, Dora swooned silently towards Jack. Swiftly Jack scooped her into his arms. 'Quick, our Madge, unlock the door, call your mother and bring the trunk.

Madeleine, now a slim five-foot female, in her early twenties, sprang into action, quickly unlocking the front door. 'Mama, come quickly,' she called frantically, as she struggled to hold open the large wooden front door with one foot, whilst attempting to drag the huge trunk into the front porch with one hand and open the inner door with the other. Finally, leaving the trunk half in and half out of the porch, she held open the inner door as Jack marched through into the hallway, swept into the front parlour and gently placed Dora on the sofa. He knelt beside Dora fanning her with a large newspaper as Madeleine ran along the hallway, calling her mother once more. '*Mama*, come quickly. Quickly, our Dora's here, she needs you.'

Finally hearing Madeleine's urgent cries, Annie emerged from the breakfast room moving at a pace generally associated with someone much younger and arrived in the front parlour slightly breathless. 'Whatever's happened?' she demanded, as Dora slowly opened her eyes.

'Sorry, I...' started Dora.

'Hush now,' demanded Annie, 'Jack will tell us all about it.'

'She had a really bad sore throat and was very tired, when we were touring down south and she wouldn't rest properly to recover, insisted on finishing the tour,' replied Jack. 'Then we were due to perform in Hull, but I had to have a doctor to see her as soon as we arrived there and he said her body was totally exhausted. It's my fault. I dragged the one I love into a world of drudgery and deprivation. Now I've half killed her.' Jack's voice rose higher in anguish and self-reproach.

'You've *both* almost worked yourselves into the ground,' reproached Annie noting Jack's highly emotional state. Struggling inwardly to remain calm, tear free and in control she started to organise everything, thus offering an element of reassurance to poor Jack and Madeleine. 'Now, our Madge, go and make a cup of strong tea, not too hot, but with plenty of sugar. Don't look so worried. She'll be fine. Jack, help her sit up properly, ready to drink tea. Oh, and Madge, when Ida arrives home ask her to make up the bed in Dora and Jack's room and when our Louis comes home he and your papa can carry the trunk up for them.' Finally, instructions given, composure secured, Annie allowed herself to embrace Dora. The two remained locked in one another's arms for quite a while.

Recovery was a slow process, taking months rather than weeks. The family doctor, a bald-headed, portly gentleman in his late forties, informed them all that Dora was extremely lucky to have survived the long journey from Hull to Birmingham for she was in fact suffering from rheumatic fever. Rest was to be a key factor in her recovery. Quickly the family rallied around to ensure that everything in Dora and Jack's room was as comfortable and pleasant as possible.

Meanwhile Jack returned to work for his old firm in Birmingham, though in a somewhat lesser position than previously. The wage was low, but enough to help towards bills. Returning to a world of perpetual paperwork was soul destroying, maddening and frustrating, but in those first few weeks of Dora's illness Jack arrived home with a spring in his step and a smile on his face. He was just happy to see his wife safely ensconced within her family, surviving and recovering a little more each day.

As the weeks crept into months, gentle exercise was prescribed in order to strengthen Dora's limbs. Slow walks in the park each day, though painful at first, progressed one day to a few wavering dance steps – in the living room – as Jack held her hands and danced slowly alongside and Madeleine played the piano. Dora's beautiful blue eyes glistened with tears of happiness as she felt her body slowly respond to the music.

Ida stood silently observing her sister as her weak legs danced their first faltering steps. 'You know I think that did you some good. You've colour in your cheeks and… well… It's time you went back to dance school. Madame Lehmiski would know exactly the right steps to help strengthen your limbs again.'

'I *like* that idea,' Dora smiled. 'And you shall come with me, to keep me company.'

'I'm there already most nights after work, except when it's family rehearsal. I could just meet you there, it's not too far. What do *you* think, Jack?'

After gently easing Dora back into her chair, Jack paused, looked thoughtful for a brief second, swiftly spread his arms wide – palms towards his family audience – in a gesture of melodramatic muse and exclaimed, 'Send *Dora* back to dance school. *My dears, darlings,* let's *all* go back to dance school. It's a grand idea. You too, Louis.'

'Me? I gave that all up years ago,' grumbled Louis.

'Only because it didn't fit in with the times of your apprenticeship when they kept you late. Your hours are less now. Come on, Louis, our Dora's counting on your support,' said Ida firmly.

Within a week of Ida's suggestion, Jack accompanied Dora to Madame Lehmiski's School of Dance, having agreed to speak to Madame for a few moments prior to their organised private family dance lesson. It seemed strange pushing open the familiar old door after so many years. So many memories escaped as Dora stepped slowly onto the worn wooden floor and spied the familiar well used piano. Jack smiled as he remembered bursting through that very same door, in a breathless bedraggled state and viewing an angel with flaxen hair playing a lively polka. His smile broadened as he recalled his shock when he realised the flaxen haired angel was indeed Dora.

'Happy days,' he murmured as he wrapped his arm around Dora's frail waist.

'It was the beginning... of, of everything,' responded Dora. 'All the hard work, the fun, the...'

'The beginning maybe, but certainly not the end.'

Madame greeted them both with a warm smile and a brief embrace, whilst endeavouring to camouflage her shock at Dora's pale drawn face. 'So, time has gone full circle and you have returned to Madame to mend you after your troubles.'

'I just want to be strong again, to dance, to feel the music,' replied Dora.

'And you will. You and Jack will be my star pupils once more. Music and dance are great healers, along with time.'

'How are our Ida and young Joan doing with their dance nowadays?' asked Dora.

'Joan's still very keen and works hard. Not in the adult class yet of course. Ida's another good pupil in the making,' responded Madame. 'Where are Madeleine and Louis? I believe Ida said you were *all* returning.'

'Louis will be here soon. He's walking down with Ida after work. Unfortunately, Madeleine's far too busy with her office work and some extra study,' Jack replied, tactfully neglecting to mention that Madeleine actually had plenty of time to attend but had no wish to do so. Whilst still participating in the family concert parties, dance lessons were low on her list of preferred activities.

Verbal pleasantries complete, Dora and Jack hung up their coats and changed into the correct footwear as they waited for Ida and Louis. Secure in the knowledge that Madame would help Dora grow strong again, both felt an initial sense of relief and comfort intermingled with an intrinsic, yet unaccountable excitement...

CHAPTER 7
A GLIMMER OF AN IDEA

Returning to dance school proved just the remedy for Dora. Madame was careful to structure her classes to include a correct balance of gentle dance steps, combined with those offering some challenge. Dora had strict instructions to sit down whenever she felt tired, but rarely did so – hence, slowly but surely strength returned to her limbs and light and laughter to her spirit once more. She and Jack started taking part in family concert parties again and even obliged Madame by doing a special dance in one of her local productions.

Despite his initial reluctance to return, Louis felt at home dancing on the old wooden floor. The music filled his mind with wonderful images and the movement filled his body with energy, fuelling his spirit of adventure, heightening the need for a real challenge, for escape. The challenge, however, remained elusive until one evening Louis observed something that would change his life forever. It all started with one of his many regular visits to the theatre. Jet black hair carefully combed, rugged face smiling, Louis and his young lady friend Jean, sat holding hands in the auditorium of Birmingham Hippodrome. Ida and her young gentleman friend Robbie sat with them.

The variety show progressed steadily and somewhat predictably, beginning with dancing girls, ukulele players, a ventriloquist and the usual eclectic range of performers, including a popular comedian. This was followed swiftly by a specialty act doing what appeared to be acrobatic ballet.

Everyone held their breath as two male dancers, lifted, twirled, threw and caught a beautiful young female dancer. All too soon the acrobatic dance finished, amid tremendous applause and the remaining acts plodded laboriously towards a grand finale.

As Ida, Robbie, Louis and Jean exited the theatre Ida dismissed Robbie with a swift, 'That was a really lovely evening, Robbie, thank you. Our Louis will see me home. Goodnight.'

'Oh, very well. I hope I may see you again soon,' replied poor Robbie, looking somewhat subdued.

'I do hope not,' replied Ida, quietly under her breath as Robbie hurried along the street.

'Oh, our Ida, you're quite cruel at times,' reprimanded Louis.

'Nonsense, he didn't hear me. There's no point in me leading him on and he's becoming far too serious. I don't want to be tied down yet or ever for that matter,' retorted Ida as Jean slipped her arm through Louis' and the three of them walked towards the Birmingham Bullring.

After wandering around rather aimlessly, they decided to board a tram back, ultimately disembarking at the park for a quick evening walk before taking Jean home.

'Hey, our Ida, come here,' called Louis suddenly. 'Let's see if I can pick you up and hold you above my head, like the dancers on the show.'

'You might hurt her,' protested Jean, rather nervously, but within seconds Ida had run to Louis and allowed him to lift her high above his head. The two collapsed on the grass, in a heap, laughing.

'That looked awful, not a bit like the elegant dancers we've just seen,' responded Jean, rather annoyed that

Louis was suddenly giving all his attention to crazy antics with Ida, when he should be arm in arm with her. 'Could you take me home please?'

Louis was silent as he and Ida walked Jean the rest of the way home. An idea smouldered, ignited and finally sparkled like a firework within his mind. He almost forgot to bid a polite goodnight as he dropped the young office clerk on her doorstep and rushed home, eager to share his idea.

Bursting into the house he removed his outdoor shoes, abandoning them precariously in the centre of the porch – ready for Ida to trip over – and ran along the hallway, in the direction of the family living room, slipping haphazardly on the polished Victorian tiled floor and flying through the living room door in a most undignified fashion, sending the door crashing against the dining table.

'Ahh good evening, young Louis. It's *you* causing the commotion,' William looked up from the game of chess he was playing with Joan. 'Do try to be a little calmer. Show some respect for our furniture.'

Joan started to giggle, 'It sounded like a tornado coming along the hall and...'

'That's enough chess for one evening. We'll continue this another time,' interrupted William. 'It's way past your bedtime, young lady. Off you go, say goodnight to your old papa first.'

Joan gave William a swift kiss on his cheek. Systematically she moved around the room hugging each person, beginning with Madeleine as she sat softly playing the old practice piano; moving on to Ida who was now seated beside her father, and finishing with Louis – still waiting in the doorway to share his idea.

'You missed family rehearsal,' she scolded as she hugged him. 'Were you with a girl? Ida missed it too. Was she with a boy?'

'Off to bed with you,' growled Louis. 'I've an idea to share.'

'With me?'

'With our Ida, Dora and Jack, but I promise I'll tell you and everyone else in the morning. Away you go.'

Joan walked quickly along the hallway towards the little breakfast room and through into the kitchen where Annie was still busy at work – having paused earlier for family rehearsal. 'Mama, where are you? Oh, there you are. Our Louis has an idea. He's going to tell us in the morning, but I think he should tell us all now.'

'He'll share his ideas when he's ready. Now run along to bed or you'll gather dark circles under those beautiful brown eyes of yours,' replied Annie in a firm voice, quickly hugging her youngest child before resuming work in the kitchen and reflecting proudly upon the progress young Joan was making at a reputable local girls' school, after working hard for the free scholarship.

Meanwhile, Louis – impatient to share his idea – ordered Ida to follow him upstairs to Dora and Jack's large front bedroom, which was now a proper little bedsitting room, displaying a few favourite ornaments, offering a desk for Jack's writing and sketching and fireside chairs for cosy evenings together. Louis knocked impatiently at the bedroom door, flung it open and marched in. Ida followed swiftly behind.

'My dears, where's the murder?' responded Jack. 'Why knock when you can walk right in…'

'What's wrong, our Louis?' asked Dora, putting aside the beautiful embroidery she had been working on.

'Come on, sit down,' she beckoned to the fireside chairs.

'We were walking Jean home from the theatre and… and… I've an idea to share with you.'

'He's been desperate to share *something* with us, ever since he came home – over ten minutes ago now,' interrupted Ida.

'Let him speak,' said Dora patiently. 'Now, Louis, you have *all* our attention. Tell us your idea.'

Finally presented with the opportunity to share his thoughts, Louis just didn't know where to start. Should he begin by explaining the disappointment and frustration he felt every Monday morning, knowing he must face another mundane week of dull routine and then tell them the terrific feeling of happiness he felt whenever he moved to music and how he wished it would never end? Or perhaps he should just dive right in, describe the exciting dance trio they'd seen at the Hippodrome and say he thought that the four of them should form the same type of act and try their luck at touring Britain's finest theatres? Ultimately, he chose the latter, resulting in awe-inspiring silence. Dora, Jack and Ida sat motionless as if frozen in time.

Ida was the first to fracture the hushed torpor. 'Am I to understand you think you and Jack should send Dora and me spinning through the air and that we should trust you to catch us?' she said, a mixture of horror and humour in her voice.

'I'd not drop you,' replied Louis with confidence.

'You may not mean to harm us, but we could end up crippled for life.'

'Dora and I have worked with some sensational adagio troupes,' responded Jack. 'The act you described is definitely acrobatic adagio dance. It's very skilled and perfect timing's imperative. *My dears,* we could *all* be maimed for life. One false leap, from the girls and us men could have a foot or knee catch us in the eye or somewhere worse... But it's a *grand* idea if only Dora was strong enough.'

'Strong enough?' queried Dora, a mild element of annoyance in her voice. 'I'm fully recovered and every bit as strong as Ida and you men! You know we can't stay here forever. We either rehearse our old act and try again with that or try something new. I say let's go for something refreshingly new. Ida?'

'It's a mad idea. Yes, I'm for it. When do we begin?' replied Ida with a laugh.

'And you, Jack?' questioned Dora.

'Then... my dears, my darlings, let the madness begin!' responded Jack, in his familiar melodramatic manner.

Taking Jack literally, Louis started clearing a space in the centre of the large bedsitting room, by pushing the bed towards one end of the long room. Ida grabbed a wooden chair and placed it in the centre of the room, stood on it and beckoned Louis to come and stand beside it. Instinctively Louis put the palm of one hand in the lower, middle of Ida's back and the other around one of her ankles, whilst Ida endeavoured to point her toes, bend the other knee and appear elegant. Slowly Louis lifted and balanced her above his head for a few moments before Jack helped him to lower her to safety.

Dora took a turn and next Jack and Louis reversed roles. All appeared to be going well until Ida took a turn, without the chair, running towards Louis.

'One, two, three up,' called Jack, prompting Ida to leap towards Louis. Momentarily she was safe within his arms, as he lifted her above his head, before he overbalanced and the pair landed with a thump on the old woven fireside rug. Thankfully both were unscathed. Oblivious to the danger, Ida demanded they try again. Again, they overbalanced, but this time an angry Annie banged on the bedroom door. 'Whatever are you doing?' she called. 'It's past eleven o'clock.'

Suitably reprimanded the four tidied the room and Ida and Louis crept silently to their rooms, but not before a whispered agreement to consult with Madame Lehmiski the next day, for guidance.

CHAPTER 8
BREAKING THE NEWS

Madame Lehmiski offered the budding adagio dancers ongoing encouragement and guidance. As soon as she was made aware of their plans, she focused each private lesson on the moves and skills required for adagio dancing. Louis and Jack were encouraged to do some weight training, in their spare time, in order to heighten their ability to lift, throw and catch the girls. Rubbing resin on their hands to reduce the risk of their grip slipping, whilst holding Ida or Dora, was also advised. Ida and Dora were encouraged to ensure they did not gain unnecessary weight.

At this point most of their rehearsals were still in Jack and Dora's large bedsitting room as it had less furniture than most of the other rooms in the house. Whilst it offered some space in terms of length, it was quite difficult in terms of height and as Jack sent Ida and Dora high in the air, across the bedsitting room, for Louis to catch, each girl would hold her breath and pray deeply not to hit the ceiling.

After several near misses, numerous broken ornaments and a few more noisy crash landings onto the fireside rug, the team of enthusiastic adagio dancers hired a dance studio, complete with pianist, for rehearsals once a week – frequently Madame would remain with them, observing and encouraging. When they weren't rehearsing in the studio, they rehearsed in Sutton Park and Handsworth Park, often watched and clapped by young families enjoying a walk together.

Within a few months the apparently unmanageable task appeared almost a possibility. By late 1931, after what seemed like years of mundane work by day and rehearsals and lessons most evenings, in addition to the studio they hired a large school room two evenings a week, to help pull the act together and Madame suggested that they took part in some of her local productions, to test the public reaction. Response was good, audiences gasped in awe, hands clapped fiercely and the four adagio dancers knew it was time to pursue their real dream, but before they could approach any theatrical agents, they needed to decide on a proper name as so far, they had simply been introduced as a *sensational adagio troupe.*

After numerous discussions, it was decided they would call themselves *Les Cygne Four* or just *Les Cygnes.* Throughout their theatrical career they were to use several different names, including the Maxellos but always they returned to Les Cygne Four or Les Cygnes.

It was agreed that Jack should be the one to write to agents, because he and Dora already knew their way around the mysterious workings of show business. Jack decided to plunge in at the deep end and wrote to one of the best theatrical agents in the business – George & Harry Foster. Amazingly they were given an audition, early one morning at the Holborn Empire in London, and informed that they had *great potential* but needed another month's hard rehearsal. At the end of that month, they were booked, sharing the bill with an artiste of good renown, playing: East Ham Palace, Palace Walthamstow, Chelsea Palace, Empress Brixton and South London Palace.

Now came the difficult task, that of informing the rest of the family that not only were Jack and Dora about to *tread the boards* once more, but this time they were taking Louis and Ida with them.

'We need a family meeting,' suggested Ida. 'It's Friday today, there's a concert party rehearsal in the living room this evening. Let's do it before the piano's even opened.'

'Surely it won't be *that* much of a surprise. We did tell everyone what we were planning to do,' replied Louis.

'I believe it may still be a shock to them,' warned Dora. 'They're all so busy with their own lives and with the concert parties, I'm not sure they realise just how close to our dream we've crept.'

Early that evening Les Cygne Four were the first adults in the living room. Young Joan was already there, complete with ballet shoes in one hand and a rather crumpled piece of music in the other.

Soon Madeleine came in, carrying a recently acquired violin. As a child she had shared lessons and a violin with her cousin. Now, finally, she'd purchased her own instrument and was happy to share her skills with the audience. Eventually, Annie bustled into the room, followed swiftly by William, his arms cradling two pieces of wood, painted red and a strange metal contraption – obviously some form of prop he'd created upon request. After putting the objects beside the piano, he started to exit the room – just as Annie approached the piano and reached to open the fallboard (lid), covering the keys.

'No, Mama,' called Dora urgently, '*don't* open it yet. Papa, don't go – we need you.'

'Don't open the piano? Why ever not?' Mama paused, right hand outstretched, as William stopped in his tracks, swivelled to face the family and then stood still. 'Family meeting?'

'Mama, we have some news to share with everyone. Please sit down,' entreated Dora.

'Oh, our Dora, are we finally going to be grandparents?' Annie's face lit up with a huge smile. She looked eagerly at Dora, searching for signs. Dora's face was certainly radiant, but somehow the atmosphere in the room, the edge of expectation and excitement replicated in the faces of Jack, Dora, Louis and Ida delivered a different message…

'Hush please, Annie, let our Dora speak,' requested William.

Ultimately it was Louis who spoke first, for Dora – absorbing her mama's longing to become a grandparent – felt as though she had betrayed one whom she loved deeply.

Louis stood in the midst of his family as they gathered around – Madeleine, Joan, Annie and William almost holding their breath in anticipation. Steadily and as patiently as possible they were persuaded to reflect on the recent local shows their *sensational adagio troupe* had performed and to consider how wonderful it would be for the whole nation and even the world to know and enjoy their act. As Louis started to explain about the agent and their first contract, William, Annie, Madeleine and young Joan plied him eagerly with questions.

'How can I explain anything to you if you all speak at once?' Louis growled impatiently.

Ultimately, with the news conveyed and questions answered – by Jack, Ida, Dora and Louis, William retreated to the breakfast room for his customary cup of tea by the fire, whilst the rest of the family started their rehearsals in a somewhat disjointed fashion, with several lapses of concentration and several mistakes. Finally, at the end of the rehearsal, young Joan announced proudly, 'As soon as I'm old enough to leave school, I'm going to dance in real theatres too.'

'Nonsense, young lady. You shall continue your studies and make us all proud,' remonstrated Annie.

'But Mama, what shall I do *after* I've studied so very, very hard?'

'You can do almost anything if you work and study hard and stay determined.'

'But if I *just* want to dance, won't I still make you all proud?'

'Oh, what a question, our Joan. You know we'll always be proud of you, whatever you choose to do. Now off to bed with you,' responded Annie, in a firm voice, as she gave her young daughter a swift hug.

Annie – taken by a
family member in
the mid to late 1920s

Louis and Ida (Idalia) practising in the park

Left to right – Jack holding Dora, Louis with arm raised
and Ida in front, doing the splits.
Reproduced with the permission of the
Library of Birmingham.
From the Ernest Dyche Collection

PART TWO
Treading the Boards
FROM 1932

CHAPTER 9
BREAK A LEG

On the 6th of June 1932, Louis spent his twenty-first birthday living his dream, performing for an enthusiastic audience – somewhere in Britain. Les Cygne Four had now been on tour for a few months. It was certainly not an easy lifestyle, but it was the lifestyle to which they were drawn. He and Ida had no regrets and were happy to be touring as a family, alongside seasoned theatricals Jack and Dora.

New experiences had been easier, because Ida and Louis had been able to share their worries with those knowledgeable theatricals. Well, *most* new experiences had been easier, but not that very first night in a real theatre. Louis smiled as he remembered the awful feeling in his stomach before their first performance – he was as nervous as a kitten, they all were, but suddenly an intangible transformation swept over Les Cygne Four as they heard the opening bars of music, a waltz from *Faust* by Charles Gounod. Louis felt the very essence of life spring within him. He experienced a terrific feeling of happiness as he moved to the music, absorbed within a wonderful theatrical creation.

On that first night, in the presence of the spellbound audience, Louis had a huge longing to convey happiness and excitement, to provide them with a truly terrific, lasting experience. His wish was granted when the audience gasped as he, Jack and Ida formed the human skipping rope – Jack holding Ida's wrists and Louis holding her ankles, turning her into a fast moving, living rope for Dora to jump over. They gasped again and held their breath, two ladies screaming, as Dora ceased skipping, stepped elegantly back and Jack and Louis turned Ida – the live skipping rope – faster and faster, finally sending her spinning into the air in the direction of Louis, as he moved instantly into position to catch her and the four drew together for their final closing pose, then joined hands and bowed. The theatre remained silent for a moment, bursting suddenly into a paroxysm of loud, endless clapping, as the audience realised Ida was safe and Les Cygne Four realised, with happiness and partial disbelief, that for the moment, they were a success.

Swiftly Les Cygne Four became known as an exciting speciality act. Swiftly they were in constant demand – playing Moss Empire theatres throughout Britain – with no time spent *just resting*. Variety shows were twice nightly with a very tight schedule and fair, but rigid rules. Standards were high, costumes had to be immaculate and acts had to ensure that they kept exactly to the specific timescale allotted – if they ran over or under that time, by even one minute, they could be reprimanded.

The life of a variety show artiste was sometimes quite solitary, because each act was simply required to perform on stage, then exit ready for the next one. They did not necessarily mingle, on a large scale, with others from the same show – unless of course they happened to meet and choose to sit together in a nearby pub after the show and Les Cygne Four were not fond of pubs, but happily they enjoyed each other's company.

Whenever they were booked for revues, however, it was different – Louis and Ida soon discovered that, in addition to performing their acts, variety artistes were required to take part in various sketches and large exotic scenes, often with spectacular scenery and props, based around a specific theme, hence whilst working as part of a close-knit team – frequently for many months on the same revue – a certain camaraderie was more likely.

In addition to theatrical standards and types of shows, Ida and Louis gradually became aware of the many unique traditions, technical terms and superstitions. A few were already familiar, from tales previously related by Jack and Dora – they already knew they would use a dressing room, enter and exit the stage by the wings, may wait in the green room before going on stage. They knew a bad dress rehearsal was meant to mean a good opening and that it was very unlucky to wish an artiste *good luck* – instead you must say *break a leg!* Ida, however, was totally taken by surprise one day, whilst chatting with a lady pianist of mature years, who was sharing the same lodgings, or *theatrical digs*. The pianist, Sheila, praised the act and said how much she liked the costumes.

'I've an idea though,' said Ida, having thanked Sheila for her praise, 'I wondered if our Dora could hold some peacock feathers, one in each hand and wave them over my head, as I rise from the ground, in the first little…'

'My dear,' Sheila interrupted, looking and sounding horrified, '*never* bring those on stage, the evil eye will bring doom to us all. A curse upon the show.'

'Nonsense,' started Ida, then stopped in her tracks, realising Sheila was truly terrified. 'Well… Don't you worry, it was a silly idea. We won't use any.'

A little while later Louis encountered a similar experience – in a dressing room – whilst chatting to a magician about his love of Shakespeare, Dickens and Thackeray. Nonchalantly he mentioned that at school he had liked *Julius Caesar* and *Macbeth*. The magician erupted into a frenzied fury, 'You dare to name *The Scottish Play*. The evil… the incantations… there will be deaths…'

'What rubbish are you saying?' responded Louis, angrily.

'He who utters that name must administer the antidote,' continued the magician, obsessive anger causing his forty-something, well-rounded face to begin to turn a horrific shade of red and his neatly curled black moustache to drip with sudden perspiration which ran from his top lip and indeed oozed from his whole face.

'Oh, come on then. Tell me what I must do,' sighed Louis, relenting somewhat as he observed the magician's ghastly state.

'You must leave the theatre, turn around three times, spit over your left shoulder and swear.'

'I'll not swear outside the theatre, there may be women there,' responded Louis.

'You must, or you must utter those famous words from *The Scottish Play*: *"Angels and ministers of grace defend us…"* and then you may enter the theatre again.'

Rather reluctantly Louis complied with the poor magician's instructions. Much later that evening he shared the tale with Ida, Jack and Dora.

'Atrocious, but you're in the theatre now,' declared Jack. 'Dora, you remember when we were playing Liverpool and Lizzie, the circus trapeze girl, said *Macbeth*? She was told to run round the outside of the theatre three times – right in the middle of that dreadful thunderstorm – *and knock* to be let in!'

'Yes,' said Dora, 'she *was* in a state when they did let her in. The poor girl was terrified of storms.'

'Well,' responded Ida, 'as Jack says, we're in the theatre now! We must expect to come across all manner of bizarre things.'

One of the first photos of Les Cygne Four –
taken by a family member in 1932.

CHAPTER 10
EERIE WANDERINGS

As their tours progressed each member of the act adopted the roles and responsibilities they would assume throughout the duration of their theatrical careers. Jack managed letter writing, accounts and advertising. He also designed and sketched each of their costumes, aided by ideas from Ida, Dora and Louis. Dora and Ida cut, stitched and created each costume. Louis then sewed on the sequins and diamantes, creating little patterns with them as he did so and whenever new dance moves and daring feats were needed to avoid the act stagnating, Louis was swift to contribute original ideas. He also did all the driving when they decided to improve their travel arrangements by buying a car between them.

Les Cygne Four's first car was a four-seater Bullnose Morris Oxford. At only five-foot-four, Louis found it rather difficult to reach the pedals in comfort, hence the front seat had to be moved forward for him, creating a convenient space behind to accommodate their large American trunk containing theatrical costumes and still leaving enough room for Ida and Dora – both quite petite – to stretch their legs. Day clothes were packed carefully into a smaller trunk and strapped to a trunk rack. As the years crept by the faithful old Morris was eventually replaced – in the late 1940s – by a previously well used, but nevertheless still shiny 1931 Packard.

Travel was, of course, an essential part of theatrical life. For Les Cygne Four and for most variety artistes Sunday was rarely *a day of rest*. Instead, it was a day of hastily locating their digs – rejoicing at the prospect of staying in a familiar house, with a familiar and well-loved landlady or despairing at the prospect of the unknown entity – perhaps he or she would smile, serve wonderful food, provide comfortable beds and running hot water, or would their host be sour, the food disgusting, the room damp, the toilet at the end of the garden, the water cold and the beds lumpy?

Sunday travel was made somewhat less stressful, however, when Les Cygne Four purchased their Bullnose Morris Oxford, for it meant the end of waiting on draughty railway platforms – the norm for many theatricals. Les Cygne Four rejoiced within their own little domain on wheels and this form of travel proved an enticing diversion from pondering the possibility of bad digs or worse still a bad first night. Their attention was taken planning and keeping to the route and finding somewhere pleasant and safe to picnic, if they had time.

On a good, smooth journey the girls, in relaxed mode, would sit at the back and crochet or read, between map reading sessions. Jack, in contrast, however, deemed it his responsibility to monitor the car's speed and as Louis allowed himself to relax and drive slowly for a while Jack's voice would penetrate the peace, as he would ask in a mildly sarcastic tone, 'Is this car breaking down?' Then, as Louis increased the speed, allowing the old Bullnose Morris to zoom around winding country lanes, Jack would shout, 'Are you trying to kill us all?' And so set the pace for each journey.

Their first journey in the car took them to Plymouth. Arriving at their destination they were pleasantly surprised to find a warm welcome, in the form of a smiling Mrs G., a widow – possibly in her mid-fifties with thick, partially dyed platinum blond hair, interspersed with large areas of dark grey. 'Come along upstairs,' she called, swiftly mounting the steep, narrow wooden staircase. 'Boys in here,' she beckoned to Jack and Louis, as she swung open a grey painted bedroom door, revealing a tiny room with two single beds, separated by a small wooden shelf. The opposite wall comprised a large wardrobe, beside an open fireplace stuffed with sacks – possibly to keep the draught out.

'That's grand,' responded Jack, shivering slightly as the cold chill of the tiny room hit him suddenly.

'Follow me, girls, in here,' smiled the landlady, pushing open a similar grey door and revealing an almost identical room.

'That's lovely,' said Dora, also shivering a little and wishing she and Jack were sharing a room. Sadly, it was often necessary for the boys to share one room and the girls another, because it was frequently harder to secure a double for her and Jack and two singles – one for Louis, one for Ida.

'I'll close the windows, the rooms will soon warm,' responded Mrs G. in her wonderful Plymouth accent which Jack was soon trying to imitate, when Mrs G. was downstairs and deemed out of earshot.

'Shhhh, she'll hear you,' scolded Dora, laughing. 'It's a really beautiful accent. I've always liked it.'

'Come on, our Louis, *and* you, Jack,' demanded Ida, 'we need our day clothes. You boys go fetch them please. Dora and I will ask Mrs G. if there's a chance of a cup of tea and hot food.'

Tea and food proved perfectly possible and Mrs G. sat chatting amiably with them as they ate.

Finally settled in their respective rooms for the night, Les Cygne Four lay drifting towards sleep.

'Was a good trip down,' remarked Dora sleepily.

'Yes,' agreed Ida, shivering suddenly. 'Dora, are you cold? I feel really cold and… and…'

Suddenly Ida and Dora lay totally still, hugging themselves in fear as a ghostly presence seemed to emanate from the fireplace and drift invisibly across the room, absorbing every corner, projecting a hazy, cold and ethereal aura. Rapidly the bedroom door rattled and the room suddenly returned to normal.

'What… whatever was that? Whatever was that?' chanted Ida in fear, whilst leaping out of her bed and into Dora's. The two hugged momentarily.

'Let's go and wake the boys. I'm not staying in this room a moment longer than I have to,' said Dora.

Grabbing warm dressing gowns, they positively flew from their room and banged furiously on Louis and Jack's bedroom door.

'Go away. You shall not hurt us,' called Louis.

'It's us. Let us in,' demanded Ida.

Swiftly the bolt was drawn open. Swiftly Ida and Dora ran into the room. Jack's head was buried beneath the covers as he moaned silently, 'No, no, away with you, away with you.'

Immediately Dora climbed into the tiny single bed, beside her husband. 'What's wrong, Jack? Whatever is wrong?' she said gently, her own fears forgotten, as she put her arm around him.

'It's nothing,' said Louis.

'Has something happened in here?' asked Ida suddenly. 'Why did you tell us to go away when I knocked. Who or *what* did you think we were?'

Ultimately, it transpired that Louis and Jack had also felt the same aura, within a few seconds of Ida and Dora's frightening encounter.

'Let's go and sleep in the car,' suggested Ida.

'That's a ludicrous idea,' protested Louis.

'Besides I don't think it's evil, it left us unharmed,' said Dora suddenly.

'Remember what our papa used to say if we were scared of the dark?' asked Ida.

'Yes, he said we'd never meet anything more frightening than our own reflections!' recalled Louis laughing.

'It seems less frightening now,' responded Ida. 'I'm going back to bed.'

'We should mention it to Mrs G. in the morning though,' suggested Dora.

In the morning, however, Mrs G. broached the subject before they did. 'How did you sleep? Did my Harry visit you?'

'Who's your Harry?' replied Louis.

'My husband.'

'But you're a widow,' said Dora. 'Oh, I see now.'

'Yes, I'm a widow, but my Harry likes to wander the rooms at night. You mustn't let him bother you. He was a good man.'

After this somewhat worrying reassurance from Mrs G. Les Cygne Four resolved to remember not to visit Mrs G.'s on any of their future tours. They also opted to search for new digs, hence later, whilst chatting with a female singer from the show, Ida and Dora enquired if she knew of any vacant rooms.

'Oh, are you with Mrs G.?' asked the singer.

'I heard she had bodies buried behind sacks in her chimneys. That's why it's so creepy.'

'Nonsense,' said Dora. 'She's a nice enough woman. It's just…'

'Well, there's space in our digs from Friday,' replied the singer. 'The juggling triplets and their female assistant are leaving early, staying with friends for their last two nights. Landlady wasn't pleased.'

Les Cygne Four never revisited Mrs G., but they did feel a little sorry for her. After all it can't have been easy having such a troublesome husband.

CHAPTER 11
BED BUGS AND RAVENS

Throughout their travels Les Cygne Four were to continue to encounter a diverse collection of theatrical digs and landladies. Most were acceptable and some were exceptional – understanding the upside-down lifestyles of artistes, in terms of work hours, rehearsals and mealtimes and offering little extras that helped to soothe distraught thespians in times of stress. One would provide hot cocoa and hot water bottles at almost any time of day or night, for female artistes whenever they were feeling particularly low. Another left home-made cakes on the table in case their guests were hungry during the night. On some occasions, however, Les Cygne Four had to contend with some quite unsavoury establishments – Mrs P.'s, in Walham Green, was one of those establishments.

From the outside Mrs P.'s appeared like any other small Edwardian terraced house in the street, with its painted wooden front door, sash cord windows and slightly grubby, slightly torn net curtains. Dora and Jack were particularly pleased to be sharing a room and Ida and Louis were happy to have a tiny single room each. Despite the overwhelming smell of stale cabbage, intermingled with damp walls and the unpleasant aroma exuding from an underweight tabby sitting on the hallstand, everyone was happy to proceed to their rooms and await the possibility of a meal at some point.

Following a rather meagre, tepid meal of congealed mince, lumpy potato, soggy boiled cabbage and stewed tea served in dirty cups, by a miserable rather unfriendly female human, they were feeling rather ill at ease. The prospect of a week living on such food and with such hostility was not very appealing.

'Never mind, *we're in the theatre now*, we must make the best of it,' laughed Ida.

'My dears, my darlings, let's go for a promenade – a pleasant stroll will do wonders before the evening draws in,' suggested Jack.

'Anything to get away from this dreadful, oppressive stench,' muttered Louis under his breath as they walked along the hall and exited the front door.

For a while they walked along the street in silence, Dora and Jack arm in arm, Ida and Louis tagging behind. Finally, Dora broke the silence. 'It can't be easy being a landlady. Perhaps Mrs P.'s short of money.'

'It doesn't cost anything to open a window or put the cat in the garden,' responded Louis. 'The smell's disgusting and the dirty cups are enough to give us all a dreadful upset stomach.'

'I say we stick it out, if we can, but when it comes to the visitor book it will be "Quoth the Raven…" that's if someone hasn't already put it!' said Ida, referring to a phrase, taken from Edgar Allan Poe's poem 'The Raven' and used by numerous theatricals as a code in visitor books, to warn future thespians of bad digs. The full line, repeated throughout the poem, says: "Quoth the Raven Nevermore".

'Yes,' agreed Dora. 'And Louis is right, windows should be opened and the cat put out now and then. *And* food should be cooked properly and guests made to feel welcome. We need to warn others, but I do feel a bit sorry for her. She looks worn out poor thing.'

That night Les Cygne Four slept soundly until Dora

awoke, at about four in the morning, scratching feverishly at her neck and then her ankles. Creeping out of bed she switched the light on and looked in the mirror. Three small red lumps sat in a row at the front of her neck. Her ankles had similar red lumps, as did one of her wrists. All were itching badly yet felt different from mosquito bites. Reaching in her bag for some calamine lotion, she dabbed each mark, put away the lotion and switched out the light. As she lay in bed once more, she felt as if tiny spiders were running across her bare shoulders and her neck. Jack stirred beside her, stretched and sat up suddenly, slapping and clawing at his chest.

Meanwhile Ida was sitting on top of the bed, in her little room, dabbing furiously at several red, itching lumps on the back of her neck and on her legs. Louis remained blissfully unaware of any troubles until he was rudely awoken by a banging on his door and confronted by Ida, Jack and Dora standing in an untidy row, looking extremely upset.

'We've been bitten,' explained Ida. 'It's, it's not mosquitos it's in the actual beds. I felt them crawling all over me, so did Dora and Jack... urgh...' she shuddered.

'I've been eaten alive too,' exclaimed Louis, as he examined his chest which was covered in small, ugly red lumps, 'but I never felt a thing. With the filth in this place, it's either fleas or bed bugs...'

'I looked in the bed, but couldn't see anything there,' commented Ida.

All of a sudden Dora sprang into action, moving quickly towards the bathroom she picked up a wet bar of soap and walked quickly and gracefully into Louis' room. 'Turn out the lights, now pull back the covers.' Leaping towards the bed Dora pounded it with the wet bar of soap.

'Whatever are you doing, our Dora?' asked Ida.

'Now put on the light again,' requested Dora. 'Look… bed bugs.' She held up the bar of soap, stuck to it were numerous tiny creatures – almost like miniature wood lice.

'How did you know about the soap?' asked Ida.

'Read about them in a recent novel. The woman used soap to catch them. We'll need to boil everything we've been sleeping in and anything near the bed.'

There was silence for a few seconds, punctured suddenly by the opening of a door across the landing, through which exited the thin, miserable Mrs P., complete with hairnet and a long, dirty grey nightdress. 'This is a respectable establishment,' she said, as she entered Louis' small room. 'Please return to your own bedrooms and remain quiet until a respectable hour. Thank you.'

'We wouldn't be here making a noise if it weren't for your wretched bed bugs,' retorted Ida. 'Look at us, we're covered in bites.'

'Never in all my years have I encountered such a disgustingly, dirty dwelling place,' added Jack. 'Your establishment should be banished forever.'

By now Mrs P. was standing, spindly legs slightly apart, hands on hips, glaring back at them all in extreme disdain. 'How dare you come here with your talk of bed bugs. This is a respectable house,' she screeched angrily, her voice almost rising high enough to break the glass mirror on the far wall.

'No respectable house has dirty cups and bed bugs. You should be ashamed to call yourself a landlady,' responded Ida.

'And your cat's digestion is appalling. She's ill and needs seeing to,' added Dora, her gentle voice raised in anger. 'We're leaving you now but think carefully about your bed bugs. You'll need to do something…'

'*My* bed bugs. I've never heard such a thing. Any bed bugs here were brought by you, you dirty theatre folk. Go and good riddance to you,' screeched Mrs P. fiercely as she returned to her room, firmly slamming the door.

'I'll not stay another moment in this filthy place,' said Louis. 'It's disgraceful. The whole place reeks. Let's go.'

Quickly gathering their possessions, including the trunk of day clothes, Les Cygne Four hurried downstairs and opened the front door.

'Wait,' said Dora, 'first we shall write in her visitor book.'

Speedily locating the book Dora reached for the pencil. Needless to say, she included "*Quoth the Raven…*" Jack then wrote: "*Itching to return…*"

CHAPTER 12
LOOFAH STEW

In total contrast to Mrs P.'s bed bug ridden digs, Mrs K. up in Leeds provided excellent, scrupulously clean digs, in an Edwardian terraced property. The only disadvantage being Jack and Louis shared a twin room and Ida and Dora shared a small room with a double bed squeezed in tightly under the window, but this was all part of their lifestyle by now.

Despite being quite poor, with a young daughter of twelve and a crippled husband to support, Mrs K. was the jolliest landlady and always seemed glad to hear about their lives in the theatre. Food was simple, but beautifully cooked and quantities were fairly generous, possibly because Mrs K. grew many vegetables and kept two or three chickens in her back garden. She and her husband slept and lived downstairs in what was once a dining room, but now served as their bedsitting room, with a tiny area sectioned off for their young daughter. This was all easier for Mr K., who couldn't walk far, as the bathroom was a strange affair added to the back of the house – approached through the tiny kitchen, via the back door, then under an arch and through into a type of outhouse, again all scrupulously clean and well kept. A third bedroom, upstairs, was used by the lodger – a retired magician.

One day Dora, having purchased a new loofah to wash with, asked Mrs K. if she would have time to soak it in warm water for her, while they were at rehearsal. The landlady readily agreed. 'All right, in a bit then,' she called as they left the front door, 'don't forget snicket next to house, it's quicker that way.'

'Let's not forget the *snicket, next t' 'ouse*,' said Jack, endeavouring to imitate Mrs K.'s Yorkshire accent, as they found the little alley between the houses and walked briskly towards the theatre.

'Jack, you're awful,' teased Dora. 'Mrs K. has a lovely accent. Perhaps we should imitate your Irish accent, it's still evident you know. Same as our Birmingham is still around a little bit.'

'Yow say*ing* I still sound Brummagem? Yows barmy yow is – stop mithering me or I'll throw yow in the miskin,' responded Louis, desperately attempting a strong Birmingham accent.

'What*ever* was that, our Louis,' scolded Ida, 'that's *never* a Brummagem accent. Just speak normally. It's mild, but it's still there. I hope we don't lose our Birmingham accent completely. Perhaps it will just fade a little as we travel *all around the Wrekin* from show to show…'

'Race you all to the theatre,' called Dora, with a sudden burst of energy, as she sprang gracefully into a ladylike run, ran out of the alleyway and onto the pavement leading to town.

'I'll beat the rest of you, you know I will,' called Ida, holding her skirt down with her hands, to prevent the windy weather causing issues as she raced towards the theatre. Two elderly ladies, standing gossiping at the edge of the pavement, gave Les Cygne Four a rather disapproving look as the four sped past them in a sudden rush of immaturity. 'Bound to be the theatre folk from Mrs K.'s,' said one.

'Aye, bound to be,' agreed the other.

Later, when they returned to the digs for their meal. Mrs K's daughter Katherine greeted them. 'Mam's a headache. She's left me to cook.'

Seated around the dining table Les Cygne Four sat in anticipation of another good meal, chatting a little with the retired magician who was seated at the head of the table. Soon Katherine appeared with a huge bowl of steaming vegetables and potatoes, placed them on the table and returned to the kitchen. Next, she came in with a plate containing two sausages and placed it in front of the magician, then placed a pile of empty plates and cutlery on the table. Finally, she brought in a large pot of what resembled slightly greyish, boiling water with a long creamy white object in the middle. 'Mam said this was yours. I've boiled it for over an hour, but it hasn't made much gravy.'

'Don't worry, I'm sure it's nice,' said Dora. 'What is it?'

'The meat you gave my mam.'

Realisation suddenly dawned on Les Cygne Four as they peered into the metal pot. Staring back at them was a boiled loofah, looking extremely sorry for itself. They couldn't help laughing. Poor Katherine looked really embarrassed. 'Have I cooked it too long?'

'Loofahs come from the sea. They're very good for washing with, but not for eating,' explained Ida.

'Loofah stew, anyone? Cooked to perfection by young Katherine,' said Jack suddenly, stirring the pot and spooning greying water onto a plate.

Soon, everyone was laughing, even Katherine. Apparently, she had never seen a loofah before and when her mother had said it was in water for Les Cygne Four she'd assumed it was part of their meal.

'Darlings, I really must enlighten you,' said Jack suddenly, 'loofahs really grow in Asia and look like huge, green cucumbers. When they're young and tender some people do eat them in some parts of the world.'

'Really?' asked Louis. 'How do you know?'

'My Uncle Dillan lived in Asia for a while. Always talking about the plant life. He was a grand gentleman.'

Katherine started to look a little worried. 'But... what shall I give you for meat?'

'We've plenty of food, with all these wonderful vegetables,' said Ida kindly.

'Yes,' agreed Dora, 'you've cooked them beautifully. Come sit down, eat with us and tell us what you like best at school.'

'Do have one of my sausages,' invited the lodger. Les Cygne Four declined, not wishing to deprive the elderly man of his food and not quite knowing how they would divide one sausage between four of them.

It soon transpired that Katherine liked to go to the library and look at books about artists. She showed them some excellent pictures she had completed, on scraps of paper. Jack, who still did plenty of sketching and never travelled anywhere without a supply of pencils, charcoal and paper, immediately gave her some of his supplies and encouraged her to continue drawing. By the end of the week Katherine had sketched each of them using the charcoal. Jack asked her if they could have the pictures. Proudly Katherine presented them to him. Dora immediately pressed a little money into Katherine's hands. 'Please use this to buy more paper when you need it.'

'No, I won't take your money,' replied Katherine firmly and proudly, 'but I will draw you some more pictures next time you visit.'

Les Cygne Four stayed with the family several times

over the years. On one occasion Mrs K. proudly showed them a wedding picture of Katherine. She had married the son of Mrs K.'s lodger and was very happy, living a mile or so away and pursuing her talents for drawing, whenever she had spare time. Ultimately, while her children were young, she advertised her artwork in local newsagents and was sometimes called upon to go to people's homes and sketch their children.

CHAPTER 13
INCIDENTS AND INJURIES

Despite the somewhat hectic, often stressful cycle of travel, rehearsal and performance, Les Cygne Four embraced each new tour with a strong element of enthusiasm. Dora and Jack were already familiar with many of the theatres and theatrical digs from their previous years as tap dancers – yet they never seemed to grow tired of revisiting old haunts, often reminiscing and sharing humorous tales about past shows and artistes. Initially Louis and Ida had been shocked by the poverty they had encountered in some cities and towns and wondered at the contrasting affluence blatantly evident in others, but as the years crept by their reactions had softened a little and they had learned to simply accept what they could not change.

Touring by car, Jack, Dora, Louis and Ida frequently marvelled at the beautiful countryside, as they travelled throughout Britain and whenever the opportunity arose and time would permit, they grasped the chance of mini adventures such as swimming in lakes and rivers – away from civilisation; picnicking on clifftops – though not too close to the edge as Louis was scared of heights; and they enjoyed horse riding if they were within easy reach of a riding centre.

On one occasion they even accepted a turn each, seated behind the pilot in a small, extremely noisy light aircraft. Despite being afraid of heights Louis thoroughly enjoyed his turn in the fragile craft which appeared to be created mostly from wood and some fabric. It was really pleasantly exhilarating as the pilot swooped and curved high in the sky.

One day, in Hampshire, whilst grasping the opportunity for some equestrian fun, Ida's rather highly strung horse reared suddenly sending her flying through the air, totally unrehearsed on this occasion. There was a strong element of panic as she landed in some bushes, at the edge of the mud and gravel track and lay still and silent for a few moments. Jack was first to dismount. Leading his horse to a nearby tree he looped the reins over a low branch and ran to Ida. Kneeling down he gently took Ida's pulse. 'She's alive. Thank the Lord, my dears, she's alive.'

'Of course, I'm alive,' replied Ida, starting to get up. 'I only took a tumble.'

'Don't jump up like that. Go slowly,' advised Dora. 'Did you hit your head at all?'

'No, I landed mostly on my right side and the bushes cushioned me. Now let me back on my horse. Did someone tie it up?'

'Dora did, now let me look at you,' demanded Louis, quickly scanning her head for any signs of bumps. 'Alright, now do you think you can manage to ride back to the stables? We'll not be doing any more riding here today. You need rest before the show and we should have you checked over properly first.'

'Nonsense, I'm not having all that fuss. Bit of rest and I'll be fine.'

Luckily, true to her word, Ida was able to ride back to the stables and after a short rest, continued the rest of her commitments as usual. Emotionally though, she felt a little shaken and as the day progressed, despite having landed mostly on her right side she felt very bruised and sore all over, but true to her nature Ida was determined not to let it beat her.

That evening, however, as they were approaching a particularly awkward part of the act, where Ida had to run, leap onto Louis' shoulders and lock her ankles around his neck, Louis stood in the usual position, right leg forward and slightly bent, left leg stretched behind with his arms open wide, but conscious of Ida's recent injury he lowered himself slightly to make her high leap a little less strenuous. Although Ida had been bruised, sore and extremely tired, prior to the show, as they walked onto the stage her body and mind responded in its usual way – her very spirit was entranced by the music, thrilled by the lights and totally absorbed with the need to perform. Hence, when Ida leapt, she leapt with her usual vigour, reached her usual height, and caught Louis' face with her right knee, causing a fairly deep gash above his eye.

Naturally the cut bled profusely, but the act continued as it should, with Ida's ankles locked around Louis' neck and Louis spinning around, spine arched back slightly to counterbalance Ida's weight, his arms still outstretched, but with blood pouring down his face, into his right eye and dripping onto his bare chest, as Ida rotated with him, her body straight, face to the ceiling, arms extended above her head and fingers pointing towards each other in an elegant position. Meanwhile Jack and Dora followed a similar routine, to the right – *stage right* of Louis.

Next, with their feet back on terra firma, Ida and Dora danced into position ready for their next spin. Jack moved with tremendous strength and skill intertwined with beautifully artistic grace and affinity with the music as he lifted and threw first Ida and then Dora. His coordination and spatial awareness were always exceptional, hence Ida and Dora always felt safe as they flew, from his arms, towards Louis, but on this occasion, both felt just a slight murmur of trepidation, for they could see Louis' face and in particular his right eye covered in blood. Both prayed that he would still be able to see clearly enough to catch them.

Their prayers were answered for Louis' body appeared on autopilot. His timing and precision of movement was excellent and despite the injury he moved with his usual speed and natural grace, judging the distance perfectly and neatly catching first Ida and then Dora amidst the most tremendous applause.

Back in their dressing room once more, Ida, Dora and Jack fussed around Louis, giving him a clean cotton handkerchief to staunch the blood and making him sit quietly before he attempted to remove his greasepaint and resin.

'I've half killed you. I'm sorry,' apologised Ida.

'It's not your fault,' responded Louis. 'I positioned a bit lower, because I thought you were tired and bruised.'

'You mean you lowered your position, without telling me before we went on? Then you've only yourself to blame. But… I'm still sorry for harming your poor eye.'

'Luckily, it's not my eye, just the bit of flesh above my eyelid,' said Louis.

'Jack's gone to fetch help,' said Dora. 'It may need a stitch or two.'

'Let's just get back to the digs, it's maybe easing up a bit now. I'm going to clean up,' said Louis.

Luckily Les Cygne Four were in digs extremely near the theatre so had not had to use the car. This tended to be the norm, with the car being used mainly for the long journeys between towns and cities or for convenience if they knew they were going somewhere after the show.

Upon returning to the digs, Jack insisted he walk Louis round to a local doctor deemed by the landlady to be, 'Good at fixing people up and not much money either.'

The doctor lived in a large Victorian house which appeared rather rundown from the outside. Inside, however, it was beautifully clean and well kept. A middle aged lady answered the door and showed them into a room obviously reserved for medical matters. One wall was lined with numerous medical journals and books and in front of the window was a heavy looking mahogany desk and matching chair. The desk was covered in paperwork and contained several pairs of glasses, neatly arranged in a row, beside several small bottles and a surgical tray lined with lint. To one side of the room a large oval table contained a number of medical instruments, in another metal surgical tray. Four wooden chairs were placed neatly against a wall.

Within a few minutes a gentleman possibly in his mid to late fifties, of fairly large proportion, supporting a head of thick grey hair and matching beard, shuffled unsteadily into the room and sat slowly down at his desk. His hands were shaking violently as he grappled for a pair of glasses, tried one pair, discarded them and tried another – his hands continuing to shake fiercely throughout.

'Good evening, gentlemen. I'm Doctor George. How can I help?'

'My cut may need a stitch or two,' said Louis, immediately regretting his words as he realised that Dr George's hands were still shaking relentlessly.

'Come closer. Bring your chair here so that I can see.'

Louis complied and sat in terror as the doctor promptly glanced at the wound, shuffled unsteadily towards the large oval table, his hands persistently quivering fiercely in a worrying erratic manner as he reached towards the metal tray of instruments. Miraculously, as he grasped the tray, selected a small pair of scissors, surgical thread and a surgical needle, his hands became superbly steady. Skilfully he threaded the surgical needle, shuffled hurriedly back to his desk and sat down. Placing the items in the lint lined medical tray, he picked up a small bottle, dexterously removed the tiny cork and poured some liquid onto a small piece of cotton wool. Skilfully, again, and gently, he cleaned and then inserted three stitches in the area above Louis' right eye.

'There, good as new. Stitches will need to come out in a few days. See my wonderful wife about the fee on your way out.'

Louis and Jack thanked Dr George profusely and left in a bewildered state, wondering at the sudden, dramatic change in his manual dexterity. Their landlady later informed them that he'd been that way since serving as a doctor in the 1914–18 war.

CHAPTER 14
OUTRAGEOUS, MY DARLINGS

Crossing the sea to perform in Northern Ireland, could on occasion be a delightful experience, but more often than not the journey was dreadful, with wild winds and choppy sea. Although well acquainted with the Irish Sea, Jack, who suffered terribly with sea sickness, dreaded each forthcoming trip and generally spent much of the passage sitting on a chair, wrapped in a small blanket, with his head in his hands intermittently emerging to utter, 'Throw me overboard, I'm dying.' To be fair, most passengers were similarly affected and were usually to be heard expressing comparable phrases of misery as the sea continued its relentless tossing and turning.

Miraculously Dora, Ida and Louis all possessed good sea legs and generally joined forces with a few similarly blessed thespians, chatting, eating and observing the savage sea, its anger fully roused as it raged against the intrusion of each vessel made by mere humans. Thankfully all journeys to Ireland concluded happily with Jack's condition improving the moment his feet hit terra firma.

Throughout their travels in Ireland audiences were generally appreciative and Les Cygne Four enjoyed each tour there, sometimes taking a few days' break in Southern Ireland, with Jack's family and friends, before returning to England. On their first tour, however, the stage manager came to see them during rehearsals. After waiting patiently for them to finish a rather hair-raising part of the routine, he approached Les Cygne Four with an extremely worried and partially annoyed look on his slim, mid-forties face.

'Whatever's wrong with him?' exclaimed Dora, as the anxious man drew nearer.

'We're about to find out,' responded Louis.

'You can't perform in those costumes,' greeted the stage manager, waving his right hand in the direction of Ida and Dora, a disdainful look upon his face.

'Why ever not?' asked Ida.

'They're not decent. Our audience will be outraged. You'll have to cover your skin – your legs and here...' he indicated their midriff.

'Would you have us run, jump and fly through the air in long dresses, clutching them round our ankles as we go, for fear of offence?' asked Ida. 'I've never heard of anything so stupid. We're the best acrobatic dancers in the business and...'

'We dress this way, because we're dancers – adagio dancers – it wouldn't be safe to cover ourselves,' added Dora patiently, 'and besides our costumes are beautiful.'

'They're not decent,' repeated the stage manager. 'It's not for me, you understand, it's for the theatre, the reputation. If you don't cover yourselves, you don't perform.'

'Why hasn't anyone mentioned this earlier?' demanded Louis angrily. 'We've been on tour in this production for weeks now, played all over England, Scotland and Wales. What's different here?'

'Our audiences are decent God-fearing people. If the ladies don't cover themselves the act doesn't go on.'

'That's ludicrous, I'll not...' remonstrated Louis.

'Louis...' warned Jack.

'But...'

'Away with you then, away with you. Let us alone to sew grand new costumes,' said Jack, suddenly shooing the stage manager away as if he were a naughty child.

'Whatever have you done to the poor man?' asked Ida as the tall, slim stage antagonist slunk slowly away, shoulders hunched, head down, muttering to himself.

'Shown authority, my dears, authority.'

'It's not authority if you've promised new costumes,' responded Louis, 'it's ridiculous.'

'It's outrageous, my darlings, outrageous,' agreed Jack, his deep voice rising to high, melodramatic tones, 'but, it'll not do us any good standing around arguing with him.' Jack's voice lowered to its usual deep pitch as Dora slipped her hand in his.

'Who's he anyway, to tell us we can't go on? We're sharing the bill with a top comedian. It's not his production,' protested Louis.

'No,' responded Dora, 'it's *not* his production, but he knows his audience and this is show business. We may be sharing the bill with a top name this week; next week we could be out in the cold.'

'Well, I say we change, go back to the digs and think of a way of solving this mess,' suggested Ida, firmly, but calmly.

Huddled in Jack and Louis' small room, sharing a flask of tea, Les Cygne Four discussed their options in earnest. It appeared an impossible task. They considered creating entirely new costumes, in the form of close-fitting blouses that attached to the waistband of elegant trouser-like coverings with elasticated ankles to ensure Louis and Jack could grasp the girls' ankles easily. Another idea was to create all in one suits, incorporating long sleeved blouse-like tops and close fitting trouser-like lower halves with elasticated ankles, but for both options the material needed to be strong and cling close to the body and the inevitable hooks and eyes and metal poppers posed a problem, as they were likely to cut into the skin during fierce movement.

'Well, which is it to be, boys?' asked Ida. 'Have you decided? Shall we all take a vote on it?'

'None of it,' said Louis suddenly. 'I'll not risk injury to you girls for the sake of morality. Besides, he only said to *cover the skin...* he didn't say which type of material. He didn't say make new costumes.'

'What are you thinking, Louis?' asked Jack.

'What do many of the showgirls wear on their legs?'

'Fishnet stockings,' said Dora suddenly. 'Of course, we can buy fishnet and run up some stretchy suits, to cover everything we need to cover. We can connect it to our existing costumes with tiny, soft, covered buttons and discreet silk loops because it's thin material.'

Having secured instructions, from their lovely landlady, regarding the whereabouts of a suitable shop, likely to sell fishnet, Les Cygne Four made their way to what appeared to be a tiny haberdashery shopfront, which upon entry meandered back into the depths of a long narrow building and was an absolute wonderland of supplies for eager needlework enthusiasts. The elderly lady was so friendly that Les Cygne Four found themselves stocking up on sequins, bugle beads and numerous other odds and ends likely to come in handy for future costumes. More importantly they purchased some strong, flesh coloured fishnet, corresponding cotton and a small piece of flesh coloured silk.

Bidding goodbye to their helpful assistant they returned to their digs whereby Jack speedily sketched a rough pattern for the body suits which would be connected to thick flesh coloured fishnet tights and worn beneath their main costumes. Tirelessly Ida and Dora used their needlework skills to create the unwanted additions to their costume, aided by Louis and Jack who threaded needles and carefully covered several tiny buttons in soft silk and created corresponding silk loops to go with them.

The end result was excellent. From a distance, the flesh-coloured bodysuits looked natural – but respectable. Now all that remained was to test it upon the public. To their delight the audience response was exuberant and generous.

That first tour in Ireland, gave Jack the chance to show Ida, Dora and Louis some of the wonders of Irish scenery, albeit in rather a brief manner. In Northern Ireland they snatched time for a train journey to the breath-taking, mystical Mountains of Mourne. In Southern Ireland they were able to visit Jack's father and of course Hilda for a few days' holiday, before rejoining the tour in Liverpool. Louis had no idea how Jack had managed to organise the extra time in Ireland or who would be covering their spot in the show, but on this occasion chose not to ask.

Inevitably Hilda fussed over them all, feeding them wonderful hot meals and ensuring their rooms were comfortable. Married life seemed to suit her. She appeared happy and relaxed, sitting by the fire, with an adorable little spaniel at her feet, as she chatted with Dora and Ida about their costumes and asked Louis about his latest young lady friend – a pretty pianist, on tour with their show. Jack's father was delighted to see his only son and the two spent much time together with their discussions ranging from Irish literature to politics and then steering safely back to literature and art. John reminisced a little about time spent courting Hilda in Birmingham and the humorous sketch he had written for one of the family concert parties.

After two nights at Hilda and John's house, the six of them travelled by train to Cork and stayed with some of Jack's cousins and an uncle. To Louis' horror they visited Blarney Castle and were informed, by John, that they must kiss the ancient blarney stone, to ensure they were granted the gift of clever and persuasive speech. Not only did this involve climbing over a hundred narrow stone steps, but hanging on their backs, one at a time, with someone holding their ankles to prevent them falling hundreds of feet. The whole experience was terrifying.

CHAPTER 15
BIRMINGHAM
TO BLACKPOOL

Whenever their tours took them anywhere near Birmingham, Les Cygne Four naturally embraced the opportunity of staying at home with their family, instead of in digs. On one such occasion, in spring 1933, young Joan – now nearly fourteen – was recovering from a particularly nasty cold and a severe lingering, chesty cough. Ida, quite shocked by her pale appearance, suggested that Joan should accompany Les Cygne Four to Blackpool – their next booking – for some wonderful sea air.

'The sea air *would* do her good,' agreed Annie. 'But I've heard some of the tales you tell of dreadful rooms and deplorable landladies. She may end up sicker than she is now.'

'Oh, please, Mama,' begged Joan, her eyes glistening with excitement at the prospect of a break by the sea and the opportunity of mingling with real theatricals.

'We've stayed in these digs twice before and Mrs N.'s a wonderful woman,' responded Dora. 'She's very clean and a good cook. Louis and Jack have one room and Ida and I another, so I'm sure Joan could squeeze into our room with us.'

'She's only small and I know Mrs N. would be glad of a little extra money,' contributed Ida.

'And what would she do, whilst you're all busy working?' asked Annie.

'Come with us to the theatre, into our dressing room and wait safely in there while we're on stage and she could watch rehearsals and tell us where we're going wrong! Could you do that?' asked Louis, smiling at Joan who nodded excitedly.

'The beach is grand for a promenade,' added Jack. 'And, my dears, we all know how many rides there are… enough to…'

'Not that we would go to Blackpool Pleasure Beach every day,' interrupted Ida quickly. 'Just sometimes, to give Joan a little fun between good healthy clean sea air.'

'On this occasion the final decision shall rest with your father when he comes in from work,' Annie replied, suddenly feeling slightly out of her depth. Rapidly disguising her moment of weakness, she immediately sent Dora and Ida to make everyone a cup of tea. And then Jack and Louis to check the coal fire in the breakfast room.

Upon his return, William pondered the proposal for a few moments, initially slightly apprehensive regarding the idea of exposing their youngest daughter to a theatrical adventure, but ultimately, observing Joan's eager expression of expectation, he relented. 'I shall need your absolute reassurance that you will all be responsible for her at all times. Now is that understood?' he asked as he faced Les Cygne Four, suddenly giving Louis and Jack additional eye contact, indicating that the main responsibility lay with them.

It was agreed that as soon as the week at Blackpool ended on the Sunday, Les Cygne Four would detour slightly – to Birmingham – before going on to Yorkshire, thus dropping Joan back home in good time for school the next day. It would be a long journey taking several hours but this was the norm anyway for Les Cygne Four and Joan promised she would try to sleep for some of it.

First, however, Les Cygne Four had shows to do in their hometown. Louis experienced a combination of excitement and fear whenever they played Birmingham – excitement to be on home ground once more and to see his family, fear at failure, of making a mistake in front of friends and family. He often puzzled over this, for as a youngster, doing family concert parties, little mistakes had occurred, been overcome and even laughed over, but in the real world of theatre it was different – well to Louis it was, to the point where his normal pre-show nerves were increased two-fold whenever he performed in Birmingham.

To make matters worse, on this particular stint everyone who knew Les Cygne Four seemed to be coming to see one of the shows. On the Monday, before rehearsals, Louis, Ida, Dora and Jack were walking through Sutton Park, snatching a few minutes of relaxation, when who should appear but Louis' old childhood friend, Tommy, walking along with his wife and a very young child.

'Hello, still throwing your sisters around I see!' greeted Tommy.

'Yes, he's still throwing us around. Taken up boxing again lately?' responded Ida, with a smile, as she remembered Tommy's face when she'd knocked him out with Louis' boxing gloves, as a young girl.

'It's good to see you, Tommy,' said Louis, as they shook hands and grinned at each other like schoolboys.

'We'll be at the late show tonight,' said Tommy. 'My mam's coming over to look after this little one. How's your mam? I haven't seen her for a while.'

'Mama's keeping well thank you. Perhaps we'll see

you and your good wife after the show,' responded Louis, immediately feeling anticipation at the thought of his school friend in the audience.

Later that day, Annie informed them that she would be there, along with Madeleine, Joan, their papa, two aunts, one of their uncles and a friend from church. Louis groaned inwardly, but his worries were totally unfounded. The adagio routine progressed perfectly and the audience responded as usual with a combination of gasps, screams and tremendous applause.

As Les Cygne Four exited the stage door, a slim figure wrapped in a soft grey coat and a pale blue silk scarf glided elegantly towards them. 'Ah, my prize pupils. You were magnificent, my friends,' greeted Madame Lehmiski.

'It's so wonderful to see you,' responded Dora, briefly hugging her and then moving hastily to one side, to allow Jack, Ida and Louis to replicate her actions. They chatted for a while and promised to visit the dance school if they had time.

Then, as they walked towards their car, Tommy and his wife greeted them.

'That was the best,' praised Tommy. 'Drop by, see my mam if you have time. She'd love a signed photo of your act. Really proud she is, tells all her friends about you.'

When they returned home that night, Louis held his breath, for it was the first time their father had actually been to see them as Les Cygne Four, though he'd seen them in Madame's local shows, before they went on tour. Their father greeted them warmly – somewhat unusual for him. 'I've perhaps never told you before… your act is most beautiful and exciting. You've all done us proud. I'm so very proud of you all.' He shook hands with Jack and Louis and patted them on their shoulders, before briefly hugging Ida and Dora, whilst struggling with his emotions, for his eyes felt a little moist. Suddenly Louis knew he'd never feel anxious playing Birmingham again.

The days sped by and soon Les Cygne Four departed for Blackpool, amidst fond hugs and farewells and promises to take care of young Joan. The Bullnose Morris edged slowly along their road with Louis and Jack at the front and the three females squeezed together upon the back seat, waving to their mother until they could see her no more.

As they edged their way slowly out of Birmingham and approached quieter lanes Jack asked his usual, 'Is this car breaking down, why are we going so slowly?' Louis grinned and allowed the car to build up some speed, to which Jack responded, 'Are you trying to kill us all?'

'Ah, happy days,' said Louis, as he slowed the car a little and smiled wryly.

Whilst thrilled with the prospect of visiting Blackpool Pleasure Beach, Joan was equally thrilled to be sharing real theatrical life with her family. Her face filled with excitement as she entered their dressing room for the first time. She was perfectly happy to just sit reading, whilst they were onstage. She adored observing rehearsals, dreaming of the day when perhaps she too would dance for a living. At one point she chatted eagerly with Hylda Baker, a brilliant young Lancashire comedienne in her twenties. The young comedienne encouraged Joan with her love of theatre and her wish to be a dancer someday.

At the end of the week, Hylda Baker, Les Cygne Four

and Joan visited the ever-popular Pleasure Beach for the final time. After going on a few rides with Joan, Les Cygne Four were ready to head back.

'She's not ready for the digs yet, are you?' asked Hylda, taking Joan by the arm.

Joan shook her head. 'I think we should all have another ride please.'

'Follow me, I'll show you all how to have some *real* fun,' called Hylda and before they knew it Joan and Les Cygne Four had been given a grand tour of the complete Pleasure Beach and experienced every imaginable ride, many of them several times. Joan was exhausted, but extremely happy. Happy because she'd had a wonderful time, but also happy because she'd finally made a decision – one that would impact upon herself and her family. After her fourteenth birthday in June she was going to give up her studies, leave school, get a normal job, work hard and pay for extra dance lessons. Then she would go for auditions and become a real dancer, just like Ida, Louis, Dora and Jack. She *had* to follow her dream, but meanwhile she had to prepare to return home the next day. Home to Birmingham, home in time for school.

CHAPTER 16
ACHIEVEMENT
AND HEARTACHE

As Les Cygne Four toured Britain, hardworking, exuberant and happy to exist within their chosen theatrical world, back home in Birmingham family concerts had gradually filtered out as Madeleine became totally involved in her office work, striving for recognition and promotion in a world still dominated by men. Annie still sang at home and for some local events, between running the home, attending church and managing her little shop. William continued to work full-time in his cousin's toolmaking firm, relaxing each evening with the newspaper, a book, or a game of chess with anyone who was free to play with him.

Meanwhile, within this somewhat calmer, less chaotic environment a young spirit thrived as she strived to achieve high grades at school and grasped every opportunity to sing and to dance – at home and within the wider community. Still looking forward to leaving school that summer, Joan was already planning what type of job she could secure, in order to allow her time to save money for extra dance lessons and for travel to auditions – hence her heart sank when she arrived home from school one day and found her mother in the breakfast room, proudly rereading a recent letter from Joan's school, extolling her virtues and recommending she continue her studies further.

'I'm sorry, Mama,' said Joan, 'I know you want me to stay on, but you let the others leave at fourteen.'

'They made their own choices,' responded Annie,

'but your school's saying you should do very well as a teacher or go on to study literature and history at a very high level.' Annie handed the letter to Joan.

'Mama, I know what it says. I like study, but I just want to sing and dance.'

'Well, young lady, I've an idea that may bide you time to do both.'

'But Mama…'

'Hush now. Listen to what I've to say. Now, if you decide to stay on at school, I'll pay you to work in my shop, helping Mrs E. on a Saturday, before your dance rehearsals. You can do some evening hours between school and dance lessons as well. That way you'll gain a better education, know how to work in a shop and have time to complete all your advanced dance exams, perhaps even pay for those singing lessons you've been wanting.'

'Mama, that's charity, you don't *need* me to help Mrs E. It's a tiny shop.'

'I need you to continue your studies and Mrs E. lost her daughter two years ago and would very much benefit from having the help of a lively young person like you. She's bad legs as well and would be glad of a sit down now and then.'

'But Mama, times are hard. There's people out of work, how can you pay me and Mrs E?'

'My little shop's always full of customers,' said Annie proudly, 'so I'll not lose out. Besides our Madeleine pays her way and our Louis and Jack send money home for you, you know they do.'

Ultimately Annie's idea was agreed and followed, hence by the time Joan was eighteen she had several academic diplomas, numerous dance qualifications, experience performing in various local theatres including Birmingham's Alexandra Theatre plus a deep and desperate desire to escape into the world of theatre.

Gradually she created a solo act that enabled her to show her singing skills and display traditional ballet along with some unique acrobatic movements. Swiftly Les Cygne Four recommended her to their agent and following an audition Joan was given a part in a forthcoming pantomime which Les Cygne Four were also in. Her dream was finally beginning.

As the pantomime season ended Joan travelled to Liverpool to begin her first real variety tour and Louis, Ida, Dora and Jack returned home to Birmingham for a week's rest. They arrived home just as Annie was entertaining two church ladies, several of their cousins and an extremely elderly aunt. Quickly and eagerly the family requested news of Joan and how she had fared in a world of seasoned theatricals.

Suddenly, amidst the human warmth and chatter, the telephone sounded. Initially it rang in vain, but ultimately Ida heard it and ran to the hallway to answer it.

'Yes, he's here. I'll, yes alright... what's wrong?' Ida asked, with concern in her voice. 'Jack, it's Hilda, she needs you. Something's wrong...'

'Coming,' called Jack, rushing into the hallway and taking the receiver from Ida. 'Hello... Hilda, no, no, no... Oh, my dear, my dear, when? We'll come as soon as we can and...' the phone went dead. Perhaps Hilda had put it down or perhaps it was a fault on the line. It didn't matter, nothing mattered. Slowly Jack sat on the stairs, with his head bent towards his chest and his hands over his ears. Silently he sobbed, for his father. Moments later, forcing himself to gain control, he tidied himself up and walked calmly into the dining room, his face deathly white.

'Whatever's happened, Jack?' asked Dora, immediately putting her arms around him, as Annie rushed towards the kitchen to make a large pot of tea.

'My father had a stroke.'

'We must go to him at once,' responded Dora.

'It's too late. He died in Hilda's arms. Nothing Doc could do. It was too late.'

It was as if a spell were cast upon the household as the family absorbed Jack's loss. Movement ceased – human action froze within the space of a second, vocal cords refused to vibrate. Then, as swiftly as the spell had descended it was removed and the family rallied round with words of condolence, instant hugs from the females and a gentle hand on the shoulder from William and Louis.

Naturally the funeral and wake took place in Ireland, but when the sad event and final arrangements were made for the sale of any property, then Jack and Dora returned home and Hilda came home with them. She seemed strong and able to cope, but Dora knew it was a brave attempt to support Jack.

Hilda faltered a little as she entered the family home for the first time since Dora and Jack's wedding in 1922. She faltered again as she approached the living room, where everyone, except her mother, respectfully remained seated, just chatting quietly, to allow Hilda the dignity of entering and receiving their love and warmth, when she was ready to.

Leaving Jack and Dora in the hallway, she slipped past the living room and followed the old familiar stone tiles along to the breakfast room and then to the kitchen where her mother was waiting, knowing her daughter would come to her there. Taking Hilda into her arms, she held her tightly for a few moments, then sat beside her in the breakfast room and just listened as Hilda told her everything.

Eventually, after a quick wash, Hilda helped her mother prepare a meal, the two of them entered the dining room together and so set the pattern for the rest of the day as Hilda kept busy, alongside her mother, caring for her siblings as she had when they were young.

CHAPTER 17
TEARS AND TOMATOES

Jack was proud of the fact that his father had been born in Scotland and still had a few family members left there. Indeed, despite his Irish accent and numerous relatives in Ireland, Jack's full name definitely had a Scots ring to it and people were often surprised when they heard his soft, Southern Irish accent for the first time. Throughout the years Les Cygne Four looked forward to their tours of Scotland, particularly the dramatic scenery linking many of the towns and cities, but there was one city that always conjured an element of trepidation within their hearts and that was Glasgow. As a city it was interesting, with a friendly atmosphere, a wealth of beautiful Victorian architecture, the River Clyde running through it and beautiful hills in the background, but Glaswegians were notoriously honest audiences, renowned for making their feelings known if they didn't like an act.

Generally, the second house on a Friday night was likely to be the hardest to survive, but all shows were a challenge, hence – just minutes before their first performance at the Glasgow Empire – Dora provided them all with some much-needed encouragement. 'Remember they're all here to enjoy themselves, ignore the jeers, even the rotten vegetables, be proud – keep going and we'll win them over.'

'That's easy for you to say,' retorted Louis, 'you've played Glasgow before. And you both survived it.'

'We survived it, tap danced till our toes were sore, but with barely a clap to our credit,' responded Jack. 'Many a good act has died a death here, my dears, died a death…'

'We'll not *die a death* anywhere, we'll beat them at their game, you see,' contributed Ida, rising to the challenge.

'Yes, we'll take the audience by storm, you'll see. We'll show them we're the best in the business,' added Louis, his spirits equally roused. And so, Les Cygne Four awaited their fate, with an air of bold determination.

First on was a popular young comedian, whose efforts to engage with the rowdy audience failed miserably amidst booing and jeers of, 'Get off – go back home to your mammie.'

Seeing his act through to the bitter end, the young comic's attempts to leave the stage with his head held high and an air of confident superiority, were somewhat spoilt as he slipped ungracefully upon a deluge of rotten fruit and disappeared into the wings amidst jeers and laughter. Next on was a singing sister act complete with tap shoes and a piano. Their voices were quite sweet, but they simply didn't stand a chance and suffered the indignity of having a whole rotten cabbage thrown at them before exiting the stage and running to their dressing room in tears.

The show continued in a similar manner until finally it was time for Les Cygne Four. Luckily the stage was swept before they set foot on it or the rotten vegetables and fruit, from the previous acts, could have proved quite a hazard.

'Smile,' said Ida through almost gritted teeth. 'Smile, let's show we're not afraid of them.'

The audience jeered as Les Cygne Four danced elegantly onto the stage, to the opening bars of their music. 'Get off...' someone called from the front row. Another directed some rather improper comments at Ida and Dora. Then... suddenly, there was silence as Dora leapt into Jack's arms and he threw her to Louis. From that point on the people realised Les Cygne Four were no ordinary dancers, they meant business – they took risks and they brought thrills. There were no more jeers and no unwelcome rotten food appeared on stage, instead the act finished amidst tremendous applause, cheers and even wild whistles of appreciation.

Upon return to their dressing room the Les Cygne Four hugged each other with sheer joy and relief. Back at the digs Louis lit a cigarette. As the only smoking member of the act Louis had rather a love-hate relationship with tobacco. For weeks he was capable of smoking numerous cigarettes after a show, then upon developing a severe bronchial cough he would stop smoking for days and days, until he was almost at the point of detesting cigarettes, then suddenly something would spark the need to start again. On this occasion the tension of the recent show was enough to provide that spark. Louis inhaled the rich smoke luxuriously and leaned back upon the small, single bed in the room he was sharing with Jack. Dora and Jack sat, wrapped in each other's arms, on the other small bed, with Ida balanced on the end.

'I see our Louis' back on the cigarettes,' observed Ida. 'You'll start coughing again in a week or so, you know you will.'

'And *you've* never smoked, have you?' teased Louis.

Dora smiled, knowing what Ida was going to say next.

'Yes, I tried a cigarette. You know I did and…'

'We know,' laughed Dora, 'but tell us again.'

'It was after I left the convent school and started doing needlework with two of the other young girls,

Maria and Elsbeth. We used to take a short break in the early afternoon and Maria and Elsbeth always had a cigarette. Anyway, one day they insisted I should have one and I didn't like to hurt their feelings, but it was awful. The end kept getting soggy and I had to keep discreetly cutting it away with my nail scissors when the girls weren't looking. It became smaller and smaller, but not from the lit end. I've not smoked since.'

'I'm sure our priest back home would be very happy to hear that,' responded Dora. 'Remember how cross he was with young Tommy when he caught him smoking outside the church, by the graveyard. Tommy was thirteen – nearly old enough to go to work.'

'Remember when the priest told you off for laughing in church, Louis?' asked Ida.

'Yes, you know I do,' laughed Louis. 'He shouted at me and then asked if I had come to church to play. I thought he said *pray* so I nodded. Then he shouted, "Well you can do that outside." So I ran out of church. Our Hilda had to come and talk to me and bring me back in to sit with her. She promised me a piece of toffee if I sat quietly.'

A few minutes later the landlady called up to them, 'Les Cygne Four, someone to see you.'

'Quite late for visitors,' remarked Louis as they ran downstairs.

'It's only my brother,' apologised Mrs H. their elderly landlady, 'he wants to know if you've an autographed photo for his wife. They were both at the show tonight.'

Les Cygne Four located a spare photograph, with all four signatures on it, chatted in the hallway for a while with the landlady's large, muscular brother and his small frail wife, before sitting at the big dining table where Mrs

H. had left them a huge pot of tea and some cold meat.

The muscular brother and his frail wife joined them at the table as Mrs H. bustled around, adding more hot water to the teapot and producing a plate of oat biscuits, freshly made that morning. Conversation flowed as the frail lady, who's name was Ellen, told them all about her early life as a singer.

'She can still sing you know,' informed her sister-in-law proudly as she replenished the plate of oat biscuits. 'Go on sing, Ellen. Show them your voice.'

Ellen rose slowly with the aid of her husband and tottered towards a space beside the fireplace and Les Cygne Four prepared themselves to conjure up a polite response to a frail warble. They were utterly unprepared for the ensuing magnificent, powerful rendition of "My Bonnie Lies Over the Ocean". As Ellen sang they could almost see the lines of age falling from her face, the joy of music momentarily restoring her youth.

CHAPTER 18
WHEN THE GHOST WALKS

By the end of the thirties Les Cygne Four had worked with an eclectic assortment of variety acts, had the privilege of performing in some top-class variety shows, fun pantomimes and spectacular revues and travelled the length and breadth of Britain several times, plus given a special performance in a French theatre, yet some shows and indeed some fellow thespians remained within their memories for a lifetime…

In the very early part of their career Les Cygne Four were on tour in a show with the immensely talented and extremely intelligent comedian Will Hay, who toured the world performing his brilliantly funny schoolmaster act. Louis considered him to be a genius of comedy and was delighted a year or so later when Will Hay became famous in films. Lucan and McShane were an intriguing comedy act to tour with – with verbal sparks flying as Arthur Lucan, in drag, played *Old Mother Riley* the washerwoman, and his wife – Kitty McShane – played the daughter. Ultimately, in 1937, they too were snapped up for films.

The hugely respected Scottish singer, songwriter and comedian Sir Harry Lauder was also a delight and a privilege to work with in 1934. Although in his early sixties his talent was effervescent as he captured the audience in the palm of his hand.

By far one of the zaniest and most unpredictably, brilliant and versatile groups of comedians Les Cygne Four had the pleasure of working with were The Crazy Gang. Both on and off stage they were known for their wild antics and practical jokes.

On one occasion Les Cygne Four were on stage performing their opening movements, when suddenly the usual audience gasp as Dora spun through the air and landed safely in Louis' arms, was followed by peals of laughter. Whilst somewhat perturbed by this unexpected reaction, Les Cygne Four knew they must carry on with their performance. As the act continued the laughter subsided, but not before Louis and Jack had spotted four of the Crazy Gang, posing in mock elegance behind them. After the show the Crazy Gang – Flanagan and Allen, Nervo and Knox, and Naughton and Gold – visited Les Cygne Four in their dressing room, apologised and invited them out. Members of the Crazy Gang were always a pleasure and tremendous fun to work with.

In 1939, Les Cygne Four had very little time or need to complain, with the exception of a few minor disagreements. Occasionally Ida, Jack or Dora would become worried if Louis appeared serious over a particular lady friend, for fear he would want to leave show business and *settle down*, but they needn't have worried for it took Louis many years before he was fully smitten by a true kindred spirit. Ida, on the other hand, was determined never to settle down. Whilst happy to date on occasion, she would dismiss each gentleman friend the moment he appeared even slightly serious, declaring to Dora that she'd never marry and run around after any man – this remained her code for life.

One day, during a newspaper interview, Les Cygne Four were asked, by a rather annoying reporter, whether they ever argued. Unhappy with their initial negative, but honest answer the reporter persisted, 'But surely with all this travelling and two of you a married couple, you must have some really bad disagreements?' he said persuasively, looking directly at Jack and Dora.

'We agree most of the time,' replied Dora patiently.

'What about the *rest* of the time?'

'Any arguments we have are quick storms. We can't afford to bear a grudge,' responded Louis growing slightly impatient. 'We'll not say otherwise just for a newspaper.'

'We have to be on good terms to survive in the business and stay successful,' responded Ida.

'Away with you now,' demanded Jack, 'away back to your office. That's enough, thank you.'

The next evening, back at the digs, congregating in Jack and Dora's double room, Ida read the local newspaper review. It read:

Les Cygne Four, that sensational family adagio act, apparently united on stage, confided that their life offstage is lived amidst torrid storms of anger. Hard to believe when you see the effortless skill with which the brothers and sisters perform their daring stunts.

'What nonsense, we never said such a thing,' exclaimed Ida.

'Absolutely ludicrous and not worth the paper it's written on,' responded Louis. 'But it's only a local rag. *The Stage* newspaper is the one we *should* worry about.'

'Well, that's the newspapers for you,' said Jack. 'But it's all publicity, my dears, all publicity.'

'Still, I've a good mind to complain,' remonstrated Ida, 'it's our family and it's our act he's writing about and…'

'And he said we were all brothers and sisters, but he knew Jack and I were a couple,' added Dora in an annoyed voice.

'I've a good mind to complain,' repeated Ida.

'But he may have a family at home and you don't want to cost him his job,' responded Dora, softening suddenly, 'he's probably just doing the best he can.'

'You always think the best of people,' said Jack, reaching for her hand.

'Well, I say we let it be, it'll not do us any harm. As Jack says, it is still publicity,' began Louis.

'But it's lies, it should be reported,' retorted Ida.

'So, you'd have us run to complain, every time we're in the papers, would you?' responded Louis, his voice rising. Somehow, before Les Cygne Four even realised what was happening, Louis and Ida's mildly heated words had evolved into their worst argument in years and had that very same newspaper reporter been present that evening he would have revelled in the glory of reporting a scene of mayhem and anger, which concluded with an infuriated Ida snatching a beautiful gold compact from her handbag and hurling it into the smouldering coal fire. He would have been aware of the silence that swept the room as Ida stood still, realised her stupidity and then rushed to attempt to retrieve the precious object which had been given to her by Louis on her last birthday. But the reporter was absent, hence the dramatic scene continued without him. Pushing Ida quickly, but gently, to one side, Louis grasped the nearby metal toasting fork, flicked the poor compact, complete with cinders, onto the fireside rug and then stamped on the rug to ensure it wasn't alight.

Les Cygne Four stood in a shocked semicircle, staring at the mess. Jack was the first to break the silence. 'Stop your outrageous rampaging. Go. Leave our room immediately or…'

'I'm going,' interrupted Louis, as he left the room slamming the door behind him. He ran downstairs, out of the front door and climbed into their faithful old Morris. Revving the engine, Louis drove until he could drive no more. Parking under some trees, he sat with his head in his hands.

Meanwhile, Dora spoke calmly to Ida. The two of them cleaned both the compact and the messy rug. Within an hour or so Louis returned, hugged Ida and tranquillity was resumed.

The next evening, however, Les Cygne Four and indeed all the variety artistes were faced with another dilemma – the ghost refused to walk or in non-theatrical terms the wages did not arrive and despite much questioning there appeared to be no explanation. Theatrical unrest prevailed; jugglers, singers, a harp player and several others came from the dressing rooms and started making their feelings known, congregating in the green room.

'I'm not singing until the ghost walks,' stated Betty the tap-dancing harmonica player.

'I'll not throw a single hoop until the ghost walks,' stated the juggler.

'And I'm not going to play a note, until the ghost walks,' supported the harpist.

'We'll not dance until the ghost walks,' agreed Jack and so it went on, each act quoting the ghostly theatrical phrase, which is thought, by some, to have originated from the tale of a Shakespearian actor, playing the ghost of Hamlet's father, many years ago. Apparently, the actor refused to "*walk again*" unless everyone was paid their overdue wages.

In sympathy, with that bygone Shakespearian actor, the atmosphere in the green room became fraught with tension as the time crept to within minutes of the first show, with still no sign of the overdue wages. Then, suddenly a shout went up, 'The ghost walks, girls and boys...' and a stranger, in the form of a young teenage girl, ran into the green room, bearing wages. She was greeted by a cacophony of excited voices in varying tones. Les Cygne Four never did find out why the wages were late or who the young girl was.

PART 3
THE WAR YEARS 1939–1945

CHAPTER 19
TOGETHER AGAIN

In 1939, within the wider world uncertainty and an element of fear crept upon the country and indeed the world until, on the morning of the 3rd of September 1939, that fear was realised. People's lives changed forever as Prime Minister Neville Chamberlain gave a BBC Radio broadcast, informing the people that Britain was now at war with Germany. After his speech were some statements, one of which informed the people that all theatres and places of entertainment would close immediately.

On Sunday the 3rd of September 1939, Les Cygne Four were in Plymouth packing and loading their trunks, ready to drive across the country to Surrey, to play Croydon. Suddenly, in the midst of their usual mildly chaotic organisation and chatter, an urgent, loud and rather husky call rang throughout the digs. 'Stop what you're doing, Prime Minister's about to speak on the radio…' Mrs A. the landlady was hunched over her worn, wooden sideboard, right hand fiddling with the volume on the radio, left hand clutching a cigarette. She puffed worriedly; her puffs punctuated by a deep throaty cough. Hurriedly Les Cygne Four and fellow guest Vince the violinist, along with Miss T. and her three dancing dogs, huddled around the radio waiting.

Later, as the speech ended, everyone stood in shocked silence. Slowly the group sat around the dining table. Endless cups of tea were made and left to go cold as discussion and speculation ran rife.

'My Lenny's only nineteen. He'll be killed if he goes. Doesn't even know how to fight,' Mrs A.'s voice faltered.

'Don't worry, my dears, it'll not last long. Hitler will fail. It'll all be over in a few weeks,' Jack reassured them all, his words issued automatically, amidst thoughts running wild with fear, fear for the future of the act, fear for the future of the people and fear for Britain.

'What'll we all do?' wept Miss T., clutching her three tiny dogs close to her. 'What'll happen to me and to my babies?' she glanced lovingly at her dogs.

'Don't you worry,' reassured Dora, 'you'll do your best for them, you know you will.'

'I'm too old to fight now,' volunteered Vince the violinist, 'but will *you* fellows join up?' his eyes focused, short sightedly, upon Louis and Jack.

'We'll do whatever we have to,' responded Louis, 'and the British will win.'

'Well,' replied Ida, 'I know what we *must* do next and that is to go home to Birmingham. Be with our family, before we make any big decisions.'

Ultimately, following fond goodbyes to fellow thespians and to their loyal landlady, with whom they had stayed on several occasions, Les Cygne Four completed their packing and climbed into their faithful old Bullnose Morris. The news of war hung heavily within the heart of each conversation and heavier still within each silent pause as Louis wound his way home, slowly at first, but later taking advantage of the quiet leafy lanes and allowing himself to build up to a fairly fierce speed which everyone, even Jack, seemed oblivious to.

Late that night, Louis, Jack, Ida and Dora were finally able to relax a little as they sat in the old familiar living room within the warmth of their family. Their father appeared a little older and thinner than on their last visit, a few months earlier. His face was drawn with worry as he discussed the forthcoming war. Their mother greeted them with hugs, plied them with hot food and asked Hilda to organise clean sheets for their rooms. Joan had telephoned earlier to say she was also on her way home and so for the first time in years Madeleine found herself sharing a room with Ida and Joan again. At nearly thirty-two Madeleine was still living at home and working for the same firm. Now responsible for the work, training and promotion of many younger workers, her days were busy and despite being a female, within an era where promotions seemed to favour the male population, her prospects were good.

Joan arrived home from her theatrical tour early the next morning and so, for a short while, the family was complete once more. Instantly a cacophony of human voices rose to heady heights as everyone shared their news and of course their worries regarding the war.

Louis and Jack were unsure whether they should eventually enlist to fight or whether they should wait and see if they were called up and indeed what the overall procedure would entail. Ida, Dora and Joan were unsure what type of work they should look for, if the theatres were to remain closed, hence much discussion was dedicated to this topic. William – now in his late sixties – contemplated volunteering his services at his old toolmaking firm as it was likely the firm's production machinery would be in demand and skilled workers may eventually be in short supply. Dora suggested that, as they were one of the only families in their road with a phone, they should allow close neighbours to use it for any late-night emergency calls, to save them having to risk running to the phone box during the night if there were likely to be any bombs dropping – that is if the war actually reached that stage. Annie and indeed the whole family felt the need to volunteer to help with the safety of their local community somehow.

For a while, despite the war, the family were happy as they fell into a rough sort of routine. It was decided that Ida and Dora could help Hilda with her dressmaking business and that Joan could spend a little time at home before securing some office work – hence evenings were often spent around the piano with Madeleine playing and everyone singing. Dora and Joan would suddenly burst into a dance – their eyes bright, their movements lively. Ida and Louis would waltz and Annie and Jack would sing duets together. Hilda would sit sewing and William would sit reading a history book whilst enjoying every moment of the family entertainment.

Ultimately, however, Les Cygne Four's family time in Birmingham proved to be an extremely brief interlude. The vibrant atmosphere within the warm family home faded a little and the old house seemed so much quieter, almost forlorn, as Madeleine no longer needed to share her room with siblings. It seemed quiet as Hilda continued her needlework and William read his book. The floor ceased to vibrate with dance, the piano was silent and Annie sang alone as Les Cygne Four and Joan *trod the boards* once more.

Quite quickly the government had recognised that the British people needed ballet, opera, variety and a whole host of cultural arts to boost their morale – perhaps even to keep them sane – hence places of entertainment were allowed to reopen. Perhaps this was also a sign of defiance, a way of proving that nothing would deny the British their right to enjoy the arts – not even another war!

CHAPTER 20
HOT PAPERS AND COLD FEET

During the war the removal of signposts on roads – to confuse potential enemy invaders – combined with petrol rationing and ultimate elimination of petrol for private use, forced Les Cygne Four to travel by train once more. Whilst always friendly towards their fellow theatricals they valued the privacy and freedom that the old Bullnose Morris had provided, yet somehow the insecurity and apprehension created, by the newly arrived and unwelcome state of war, strengthened the potential to bond with other acts as they travelled together, shared train compartments and exchanged news and worries.

High on the agenda was the creation of the Entertainment National Service Association (ENSA) which was created, at the beginning of the war, to entertain the troops in Britain and overseas. Several comedians, musical acts and young female dancers, known to Les Cygne Four, had already joined ENSA and others were thinking about it.

Les Cygne Four did eventually agree to do two fairly long tours with ENSA, in the early days of World War Two and travelled aboard coaches full of ENSA entertainers – with any necessary props stored beneath each coach – earning far less money than they had as a speciality act in normal variety and revue, doing their bit to help with the war. But in November 1939, with pantomime season approaching, followed by a contract for a long tour that had to be completed, they remained in mainstream theatre, knowing, of course, that Louis and Jack could be called up to physically fight and perhaps even the girls at some point – if the war lasted.

For the moment they would continue to entertain the people of Britain and later accept their duty to defend their country if needed. Meanwhile the train journeys continued and as the war persisted almost everyone seemed to have someone dear to them who was either fighting, injured or even worse, hence on some journeys there seemed to be a need to instigate a lively, uplifting atmosphere within the train carriage, which could, at times be taken to extremes...

On one occasion the men were nattering quietly in one corner of the compartment, Louis working on a small tapestry; Jack drawing the passing scenery, whilst secretly longing to sketch the bespectacled, strict and extremely solemn face of Miss Belinda, the slim, elegantly dressed middle-aged female singer sitting in the far corner of the compartment and reading a large newspaper – Jack was itching to exaggerate each human line into a comical masterpiece. Opposite Jack and Louis an elderly gentleman commented on the weather from time to time, whilst Ricardo, a lively tap-dancing comedian, known for his wild and bizarre sense of fun, sat looking extremely bored as he puffed on a long, elegant cigarette holder between conversation with Jack and Louis.

Suddenly, a wicked gleam glistened within Ricardo's eyes as he put down his cigarette holder, gently nudged Louis and Jack and whispered, 'Watch me, boys...' and before they could stop him, Ricardo – lit cigarette lighter in hand – crept stealthily across the floor, lit a low corner of the large newspaper, just as its reader was enjoying a particularly interesting piece of news and totally unnoticed by Dora and Ida as they sat opposite quietly chatting with a female contortionist.

Louis and Jack observed, with a mixture of excitement and horror, as the faint flick of a spark became a small flame – gradually consuming the lower section of the large newspaper and working its way up the side, totally unnoticed by Ida, Dora, the contortionist or indeed the newspaper reader herself, until Ricardo – now innocently sitting back with Louis and Jack once more – called out, 'Excuse me, Miss Belinda. Is your newspaper *hot off the press?*'

'I beg your pardon,' replied Miss Belinda, with a disapproving frown, annoyed at being disturbed.

'Your newspaper, is it *hot off the press?*' repeated Ricardo, just as the flames started to grow a little and Ida, Dora, plus the contortionist realised what was happening and just as poor Miss Belinda, feeling a certain flickering warmth above her knees, glanced down, screamed and flung the burning paper onto the floor.

With the exception of the elderly gentleman who had now fallen asleep and was snoring loudly, everyone leapt into action, including the culprit. They stamped on the burning paper, deftly defeating the flames. Ricardo continued stamping on the paper, long after the flames were quenched, finally doing a strange little tap dance. Then, neatly sweeping the ashes to one side, with his right foot, he examined the floor of the train with a look of mock concern, gave a little nod of comic approval and then returned to his seat.

'Whatever possessed you to do that?' asked Louis, his voice caught midway between laughter and shock.

'Just to brighten the journey,' responded Ricardo.

Dora, Ida and the contortionist couldn't prevent

themselves laughing at the practical joke before they comforted a rather angry and distressed Miss Belinda.

'That *was* a rather foolish thing to do,' commented the contortionist.

'Ah, but you must agree, I can always spark life into the quietest of people,' replied Ricardo, with a wide smile. He then sat silently smoking his cigarette for the rest of the journey – his need for excitement apparently extinguished.

Arriving at their digs extremely late that evening, due to an air raid just as the train pulled into the station, Les Cygne Four were greeted with further, rather unwelcome chaos, as Mrs B. the landlady called them to one side. 'Mrs S. in the High Street's been bombed out and...'

'Oh dear,' replied Dora. 'Is she... alright, did...'

'Oh, she's fine, naturally she's shaken up. She's gone to her mum's for now, but she's asked that I take her three guests. Boys, you've two in with you, both on folding put-you-ups.'

'That's grand, my dear,' said Jack. 'Anyone we know?'

'Didn't catch their name. Cycling twins, playing at the other theatre from tomorrow. And, girls, there's a girl at the foot of your bed, in a put-you-up. Said she's joining your show tomorrow, so good for you to meet her.'

'She'll be the replacement for Doreen,' responded Dora, referring to a young girl whose relationship with a soldier had resulted in the need for her to marry in rather a hurry.

'Who are we getting?' asked Ida.

'Not sure, but we're about to find out,' responded Dora. 'Mrs B's right, it'll be nice to meet her.'

Having settled Jack and Louis in their room, Ida and Dora crept into their bedroom, expertly unpacked a few essential items by torchlight – to avoid awakening the tousle-haired sleeping girl, in the put-you-up – then tiptoed quietly along to the bathroom. They washed down in tepid water and slipped silently back to their room. Both sisters shivered as they climbed into the double bed and dived beneath the covers.

'Something to eat would have been welcome,' whispered Ida.

'I couldn't have faced supper downstairs, this late,' replied Dora, 'just as well we took some food on the train though. Must remember to hand her our ration books is the morning or there'll be no food.'

'It surely wouldn't have hurt Mrs B. to leave us a tiny bit of left-over supper, even if we are late. And a hot cup of tea would have warmed us up a little.'

'Some hope. This isn't the Ritz,' responded Dora. 'And three guesses what they had for supper.'

'Cabbage,' whispered Ida, lifting the covers a little and sniffing the all-familiar smell of stale cabbage. 'Why do so many digs smell of stale cabbage?'

'Perhaps it's cheap to buy or easy to cook. And easy to forget to open up some windows and let the smell out. Oh, for some meat and vegetable stew, just like our mama cooks.'

'And a bread-and-butter pudding, like our Hilda makes.'

'Yes, but "*There is a war on you know*",' responded Dora, smiling silently beneath the covers. 'Oh well, best sleep now, we don't want to wake sleeping beauty over there.'

A few moments passed as Dora and Ida drifted towards a dreamy sleep. All was peaceful until an urgent whisper, from Ida, punctured the silent darkness. 'Did

Mrs B. say she put a hot water bottle in the bed?'

'I doubt it.'

'Well, I think there's a cold, stone water bottle near my feet. It's horribly cold.'

'Then move your feet.'

'But... but I think it moved. Should it move?'

'No, I don't think so...' replied Dora sleepily. 'Keep it over your side anyway, I don't want cold feet.'

'Ahh, it's mooooving... urgh, quick, put the light on, put the light on...'

Both girls leapt out of bed and screamed as Dora switched on the light to reveal a moving mass beneath the covers of the bed.

Just then a soft, sleepy Irish voice demanded to know what was happening.

'There's... there's something in our bed. It's moving.' Ida – fear and disbelief upon her face – pointed towards the bed covers which appeared to be moving restlessly in waves, apparently having a fight with themselves.

Pulling back her covers and climbing out of her folding bed, the owner of the beautiful Irish accent – a pretty dark-haired girl in her twenties – looked towards Dora and Ida, her brilliant blue eyes glistening with amusement. 'Stand back, ladies,' she commanded, 'now don't you be worrying about a thing. It'll be one of my girls bothering you. They just love to curl up inside a lovely warm bed.' Speedily the young girl whipped off the blankets and there, towards the bottom of the bed, was a huge red-tailed boa constrictor approximately seven to eight foot in length.

'Oh dear, whatever will happen next?' gasped Ida. 'Now I know you, you're Sheila the Snake Queen, the girl who dances with snakes. You played in *Aladdin* with us, the other year.'

Sheila nodded apologetically. 'That's me. Come along now, Betty.' Swiftly and lovingly, she scooped up the enormous snake and hung it around her neck, holding its lower end carefully with her left hand.

Just then, the wardrobe door creaked open and a second enormous boa constrictor slithered gracefully onto the floor.

'Come along now, Bettina, you naughty girl. You're both such disobedient girls to escape from the wardrobe. If you come out again, I'll have to put you in your sleeping baskets.'

Dora and Ida exchanged horrified looks and with one accord leapt back into their bed, tucking the covers firmly around them and over their heads. The following day they managed to persuade Sheila to lock the boas in the bathroom each night. As the toilet was separate, this worked quite well. Both snakes curled up on some towels in the bath and Sheila said they were really quite comfortable there. Somehow Les Cygne Four felt comfortable too, knowing that both snakes were a few doors away!

CHAPTER 21
NARROW ESCAPES

Bravery seemed to be part of everyday living for many people during the war, not least those dwelling within areas of strategic importance to the enemy, such as main cities and ports, hence Les Cygne Four were privileged to witness and indeed become part of that bravery and British spirit as they travelled throughout Britain. On more than one occasion they arrived at digs to discover the landlady cooking a basic meal for her guests, whilst comforting a friend or neighbour who had just received news of a loved one injured or killed in action. Several times they encountered displays of unwavering courage as landladies cared for their families and guests, whilst nursing tremendous fear awaiting news of a young son or husband missing in action.

In many areas of the UK, a more friendly caring spirit appeared to evolve and in London, where countless people slept in the Underground stations to stay safe during the bombing, Les Cygne Four were used to weaving their way around people's makeshift beds. Often, they would see and hear families singing together on the platforms and the odd accordion playing as people used music to strengthen their spirits or perhaps simply to unite in defiance of the enemy.

The enemy was certainly visibly present in Portsmouth one afternoon, as Ida and Dora made their way towards the theatre, for their matinee performance. Their digs were not far from the docks and as they walked along the pavement, towards the town, the air raid siren offered its eerie, melancholy cry. A young couple and some stray children disappeared from the street – presumably seeking safe shelter – but Ida and Dora continued briskly, determined to reach the theatre before their show began.

Within seconds of the siren, explosions were heard coming from the dockyard and nearby buildings and within seconds a fighter aircraft swooped over the rooftops. Flying low it started firing at Ida and Dora. Dora grabbed Ida's hand, 'Run for your life! Run, Ida, run!' Clutching hands, they ran.

Relentlessly the plane followed and relentlessly the pilot fired at the two innocent humans. Suddenly, a bus sped along the road at top speed – the middle-aged driver desperately trying to take his passengers to safety. Miraculously, he slowed the bus for a split second as he drew near to them and within that split second the heroic conductress leaned out of the open doorway and pulled both Ida and Dora roughly onto the bus. Both landed in a heap on the floor as the conductress rang the bell and the bus regained its frantic pace once more, pursued by the fighter aircraft firing along the way. Then, as quickly as it had appeared, the aircraft disappeared up into the clouds.

'Alright?' asked the conductress, addressing Ida and Dora as the bus slowed its hectic speed a little. Both nodded, their faces and those of many of their fellow passengers pale with shock.

'We owe you our lives,' said Ida, successfully steadying her voice. 'We can't thank you enough.'

'And your driver,' responded Dora, 'tell him we'll not forget his bravery, slowing the bus for us and yours as you pulled us out of harm's way.'

'Only a slip of a girl she is too,' interrupted an elderly female passenger, pointing to the conductress, as the bus drew to a halt, to let some passengers disembark. Ida and Dora thanked the conductress again, jumped down and ran the rest of the way to Edinburgh Road Coliseum Theatre – once known as The Empire Palace.

Meanwhile Jack and Louis were pacing the dressing room, praying that Ida and Dora would stay safe during the raid. Suddenly both sisters burst in, pale, breathless and with a few minor cuts and bruises from their recent encounter with the floor of the bus.

'My dears, darlings…' Jack's deep voice rose as he drew Dora to him in a close embrace.

'Whatever's happened to you both?' asked Louis, his voice wedged somewhere between joy and concern – joy at seeing them, concern for the state they were in.

After a brief explanation, Ida and Dora covered most of their small cuts with greasepaint, the show started and when it was time for Les Cygne Four to perform, spurred on by sheer adrenaline, they gave their usual strong performance, finishing amid appreciative applause.

That evening Les Cygne Four were subjected to further shocks during their early evening performance, for as the show progressed merrily, with some excellent audience response, abruptly, another heavy air raid attempted to interrupt the momentum. By now, of course, theatricals were accustomed to performing amid the muffled sound of bombs and planes, particularly when playing in the major cities and ports.

Audiences were quite well informed – via posters and programmes – regarding what to do in the event of an air raid. Very often, though, the theatres remained pretty full during raids. Whether this was due to the enthralling talent of the artistes – or simply the fact that many of the people felt safer and partially distracted from the dangers of war, as they sat in the theatre – will possibly never be known, but on this particular occasion, in Portsmouth, most of the audience remained and the entertainment continued.

When it was time for Les Cygne Four to begin their routine the dampened drone of the planes seemed to accentuate the danger of the spectacular adagio dancing and the audience sat enthralled as Ida and Dora spun through the air. Each time a bomb exploded the people gasped and their heads followed the sisters, as they reached awe-inspiring heights, terrified lest the threat overhead should cause Jack or Louis to commit a fatal error.

In the final seconds of the routine, with alarming timing the sound of bombing heightened as the threat drew nearer to the theatre. The building seemed to tremor. Instantaneously the lights went out – just as Jack threw Ida towards Louis. Ida was left gliding through the air, in total blackness. Louis, his heart pounding, as if it would explode, forced his arms into position to catch her, hoping and praying his judgement was correct. He waited, not daring to move. Mercifully, as always, Jack had thrown Ida with skill and precision, Louis felt a familiar weight drop into his arms and as if by magic the lights came on again, allowing everyone to see Les Cygne Four in their final graceful positions.

Later, one of the stagehands, who had been sneaking a look at the show from the wings, plucked up the courage to speak to Ida. 'Weren't you scared, alone up there in the dark?'

'A bit,' responded Ida. 'But I knew our Louis would catch me.'

This narrow escape played a good part in some fresh publicity. In fact, one, possibly slightly deranged, lesser-known, agent approached them two days later with a proposition. 'I'll sign you up for a year, with the prospect of immediate booking – one condition, the *lights off and on feature* is included as part of the act,' he said, as he looked directly at Jack and Louis – totally ignoring Ida and Dora.

'Are you mad? Do you bear me a grudge, or do you just want to kill the whole act?' Ida's response was swift and angry.

'I've never heard such a ludicrous idea,' contributed Louis, an angry edge to his voice.

'We've no need of a new agent,' added Dora, firmly. 'We've a long contract in this revue and we're loyal to those who are good to us.'

'But think of the wonderful extra thrill, darlings, work would flow in,' persisted the agent.

'Work *is* flowing in – we're wanted all over the world,' replied Jack, in a melodramatic tone, exaggerating a little as he faced the agent, arms outstretched and palms forward. 'Now, thank you, but we're grand. You've had our answer, now away with you.'

'Well,' replied Louis, as the poor agent exited the room with great alacrity, 'I don't think he'll bother us again! Not sure about the "wanted all over the world" though. We went to France, before the war, but…'

'Ahhh, but we would be, *but there is a war on you know.*'

'You've an answer for everything,' laughed Louis.

On a more sombre note, the fierce bombing during their show in Portsmouth caused much damage. Some families lost their homes within seconds and there were high fatalities that evening – leaving many people to rebuild their lives and carry on as best they could.

Left to right – Back: Louis, Jack. Front: Ida, Dora

CHAPTER 22
CITY OF FLAMES

Travelling to and from performances, either on foot or by bus, frequently involved danger from air raids. In March 1941, whilst playing The Alexandra Theatre in Kingston Upon Hull, as Ida and Dora were returning home from an evening performance, followed closely by some of the young chorus girls who were staying in various digs in the same road, the unwelcome howl of the air raid siren was already infiltrating the air, denying the girls a safe and peaceful, if rather chilly, walk home.

The dark evening sky was alive as bombs dropped and shrapnel flew through the air – one piece missed Ida's head by inches as she ran. 'You'll not get me,' she yelled, shaking her fist at the sky in anger.

'It's too close,' shrieked one of the chorus girls, as they ran along the heavily built-up street, 'we'll never make it back.'

'Stop, Betty's fallen over,' screamed a girl, as she paused to help her friend.

'We must keep together,' called another. 'Follow Les Cygnes.'

'Let's hold each other's waists and run together,' suggested Dora, firmly organising the young girls, ensuring those carrying their gas masks looped them over their arms – thus leaving hands free to hold onto someone.

Wildly they ran along the uneven, war-torn streets, clinging onto each other amidst other pedestrians seeking shelter. As they reached one road people called to them, 'Come to our basement, quick. There's room,' but Ida and Dora refused to stop.

'Everyone's gone to the basements – look, we're the only ones,' called one of the chorus girls.

'We'll not stop, until we reach the digs,' shouted Ida.

'Keep with Les Cygnes,' yelled Betty. 'They'll be safe.'

Eventually they reached the comparative safety of their respective digs. Ida and Dora flew through the front door and into the arms of Louis and Jack who were pacing the floor of the hallway, waiting for them.

'My darlings, praise the Lord,' exclaimed Jack as he held Dora close to him.

'It's madness out there,' ventured Ida, steadying her voice as she entered the dining room and sank onto a dining chair. 'Why are you both downstairs?'

'Everyone's in the cellar,' responded Louis, pointing towards a cellar door in the hallway. 'Mrs L. said if we must stay in the main house then to stay downstairs and shelter under the table.'

'And so, you paced the hallway instead,' said Dora, kissing Jack.

'Did Mrs L. leave us any supper?' asked Ida.

'On the table still. Let's eat,' replied Louis, as he lifted the metal lid from a large pot.

'I need to clean myself up first. I feel drenched in dirt and dust,' responded Dora. 'We can eat in a few minutes, unless of course you want to go to the cellar.'

'Never,' retorted Ida. 'I'll not risk being stuck there for good.'

'If we're going to die, we'll die anyway, whatever we do,' added Louis, sharing a somewhat illogical philosophy regarding personal fate.

After their meal, Les Cygne Four went upstairs to sleep, despite the heavy bombing still apparent outside. Twice they were thrown out of bed by the vibration of nearby bombs. Finally, unable to settle, they fumbled for the light switch on the landing, discovered the power was down, hence made their way downstairs in total darkness, first into the dining room and then into the kitchen.

Powerless to see what was going on outside, due to the combination of painted black cardboard on some windows and standard blackout curtains on others, Jack tentatively opened the back door to peer out. The noise was horrendous with gunfire, aerial bombardment, crashing of buildings, screams, shouts and barking dogs. Looking down towards the city, Les Cygne Four saw a glowing mass of orange and yellow flames, feasting on buildings and flickering towards the sky. An overpowering smell of burning wood and raw sewage intertwined with plaster dust as plumes of smoke entered the kitchen.

Jack shut the door firmly. Silently Les Cygne Four crept under the dining room table and sat together holding hands, until sometime after four in the morning when the all-clear siren sounded and Mrs L., the landlady, her two children and a young magician, returned from the cellar, cold, damp and tired.

That same morning an air raid warden knocked on all the doors in the road and warned the men not to let women and children go out. 'Why ever not?' asked Ida.

Louis, who'd spoken with the air raid warden, knew there was no easy way to explain so he simply related the truth. 'There are bodies that need clearing.'

Jack, Dora and Ida were silent.

'We should phone home again soon,' said Dora suddenly. 'See how things are in Birmingham.'

'Mrs L. hasn't a phone,' replied Louis, 'lines are probably down anyway. Maybe try tomorrow.'

Later that morning Louis and Jack ventured out to discover whether the theatre was still standing. Remarkably The Alexandra Theatre in George Street stood tall and proud, amidst the rubble.

In the evening, as Les Cygne Four made their way to their six o'clock performance, Ida and Dora passed the road where kind people had called out to them and to the chorus girls, to welcome them into their shelters. There was nothing there but rubble – no sign of life and no way of knowing if anyone had survived. Despite their usually tough personas, both Ida and Dora had tears in their eyes as they thought about the frailty of those innocent human lives in the face of war.

During the war, for security reasons, exact locations of severe bombings tended to be avoided – for example a news report may mention *severe bombing in a Northern Coastal town* rather than *in the Port of Kingston upon Hull*, but when Les Cygne Four heard the news of extremely severe damage to a Northern Coastal town, some weeks later, somehow they knew it was Kingston upon Hull and they prayed silently for the poor people they had known.

History now confirms that – in May 1941 – heavy raids destroyed The Alexandra Theatre and most of the city of Hull. Buildings crumbled into rubble and flames leapt high, leaving the people with much heartache and devastation to overcome. Hull's physical appearance changed forever, but the brave spirit of the people remained as they fought to survive amidst the ruins.

CHAPTER 23
TIN HATS AND LIGHTS OUT

Birmingham's important industrial status – manufacturing tanks, planes, army vehicles and weapons – made it the target of much heavy bombing and Les Cygne Four were often shocked by the state of their poor city when they returned home to play the theatres there. They performed at Aston Hippodrome in April and September 1940, in June 1941 and in November 1943 and each time there were fresh changes to note. Families they'd known, who had lived in the same streets for generations, were nowhere to be found – their houses flattened. A boy Ida had been quite fond of, as a teenager, had gone to war and was missing in action and one of their mother's elderly church friends, whom Louis remembered plying him with cups of milk and cakes as a young boy, had been killed in an air raid. Upon each return the list grew. Whilst their mother was able to inform them that many of the families they'd known had survived – a number now in fresh accommodation – sadly several old familiar faces would not be encountered again.

On one occasion Les Cygne Four arrived at their old home to find it devoid of human life. Louis knocked on the front door several times, but to no avail. 'Where is everyone?' he growled. 'They knew we were coming home today. Anyone have a key to hand?'

'I've mine,' responded Dora. 'It's in with my gas mask.' Carefully she unlocked the front door and stood aside to allow Louis and Jack to heave the heavy trunks through the porch and into the hallway.

'Now, you boys, shoes in the porch,' directed Ida, 'you know Mama likes slippers indoors. You can wash in the kitchen. Dora and I will freshen up in the upstairs bathroom. Then I'll make us all a nice cup of tea.'

'And I'll see if Mama has left us a note somewhere,' added Dora.

A few minutes later, Louis and Jack, suitably relaxed in the living room, awaited their tea. Within seconds Ida appeared with a tray ladened with cups, saucers, a full teapot and milk jug.

'There's no sugar and the milk's powdered. I didn't want to use the small amount of milk left in the larder.'

'There's a note from Mama,' called Dora, running along the hall waving the handwritten message. 'It was on the table in the breakfast room. I'll read it out, shall I?' Swiftly she sat beside Jack and proceeded to read the following simple message:

Dear Louis, Dora, Jack and Ida,

Madeleine is doing special training and then evening duty with the Air Raid Precautions (ARP). Hilda is helping at the Emergency Rest Centre. I'm helping at the church for a little while today and your father is cleaning some of the equipment at his old firm, ready for Monday. We will all be home as soon as we can and very much look forward to seeing you.

Your loving mother

'I can't get used to our mama calling herself *mother* whenever she writes to us. I know she's been doing it for years now, but I still think of her as Mama. I'm fine calling Dada Pa though, seems normal somehow,' remarked Dora.

'Me too,' agreed Ida. 'Pa's fine, but I can't bring myself to say mother.'

'So, what exactly does Hilda do at this Emergency

Rest Centre?' asked Louis.

'She's not been there long,' replied Dora, 'but on the phone, last week, she said that because of clothing rationing, she can't do much dressmaking or tailoress work, so she's working at Mama's shop some days and doing voluntary work the rest of the time – even at weekends. She's needed to help cook food and give clean clothes to people who've lost their homes from bombing.'

'Thought it was something like that,' replied Louis. 'I can just imagine our Hilda cooking mountains of food for everyone. Luckily, she's in her forties now so she probably won't be called to do any other war-time work.'

'I'm worried about our pa giving so much time to his old firm,' mused Ida. 'I know there's a shortage of skilled workers and he's training many of the women, but going in to clean the machinery on a Sunday is too much for him.'

'He looked very frail last time we saw him,' agreed Jack. 'I hope Madge comes in wearing her ARP uniform, we haven't seen her in it yet. She'll be a force to be reckoned with – all five-foot of her, in that tin helmet.'

One by one William and Annie and Hilda arrived home and by early evening the family were sitting around the living room table eating a typical war-time meal, with very little meat, but plenty of potato, followed by homemade cakes made with powdered egg and containing grated carrot to sweeten them. Finally, after washing up, they gathered around the piano to sing. Dora played for a little while, then encouraged her mother to carry on, whilst she waltzed with Jack as the others sang.

Dora's eyes danced with light and laughter as she and

Jack whirled around the living room, in perfect time to the music. 'Oh, it's so lovely to be back home for a week, even if there is a war on.'

'At least Hitler hasn't destroyed Aston Hippodrome yet,' responded Louis. 'Let's hope there's a good turn out tomorrow.'

Suddenly, as if in defiance of Louis' mention of Hitler, the air raid siren sounded. Annie stopped playing. 'Down in the cellar, everyone.'

'But on tour we never go in cellars or air raid shelters,' said Ida.

'I'll have none of that nonsense this time,' replied William firmly. 'You know we go in the cellar. It's by far the saf—' His sentence was cut short by the most tremendous explosion that shook the house, causing all the doors to burst open. As the front door flew open, an elderly policeman on his hands and knees, rapidly followed by a young lady thrown full length onto her right side, clutching frantically at the walls with one outstretched arm, swept through the polished tiled hallway, past the open parlour and living room doors right through the breakfast room and the kitchen into the back garden. They landed unceremoniously, in a tangled heap, the elderly policeman rather embarrassingly intertwined with the young lady lying on top of him.

Time appeared to freeze for a moment, as the family, shocked by the explosion and mesmerised by the vision of two unexpected visitors gliding through their home, stood as statues, mouths partially open in surprise. Ida broke the spell. 'Wherever did *they* come from?'

'Best go and see if we can help them,' responded William, 'Come on, Annie, you know a little first aid.

The rest of you, go into the cellar.'

Annie rushed towards the rather ungainly couple, as they were struggling, somewhat tentatively, to untangle themselves, mindful of any possible injuries they may have.

Annie helped the young lady to her feet, observed a deep gash on her right leg, but no other apparent injuries, whilst William carefully checked the elderly policeman, offered him his hand and pulled him to his feet. Both visitors were helped into the breakfast room, whilst Annie cleaned and bandaged the lady's leg.

'Do you think you could make it into our cellar, to shelter until the raid's over?' asked William amidst the sound of heavy bombing.

Both nodded and allowed themselves to be helped down the steps, into the rather unwelcoming, cold, damp basement, furnished simply with one old table upon which were placed small tins of tea, a tea strainer, teapot and powdered milk, several tin cups, three spare torches, candles, matches and a small pile of blankets. In addition were two large flasks of boiled water. Between her numerous tasks each day Annie was responsible for replenishing these with freshly boiled water, thus ensuring that, whenever an air raid occurred, they were at least able to make a pot of tea. Beside the table were a few wooden chairs and an old armchair.

The young lady was now crying uncontrollably. Annie helped her to the old armchair and Dora prepared a cup of tea. She put her arm around her. 'It's alright, you're safe now. Here, drink some tea. I'm Dora. What's your name?'

'Catherine,' whispered the young lady, amidst sobs.

'Don't you worry, Catherine. We'll not be hurt down

here. It'll all be over in no time.'

Catherine sipped the warm tea gratefully and appeared reassured. 'I was just walking home from my mam's, when the air raid sounded.' She glanced across at the policeman and smiled. 'Oh, dear we did land in rather a heap, didn't we? Are you alright?'

'I'm alright… too old for all this. I was meant to retire last year, but this war…' the policeman paused. 'Still, I'm luckier than the young ones, having to go to fight.'

'You simply shot along the hallway,' Jack's face bore the beginning of a smile, 'like a dog on all fours after a—'

'Jack,' warned Dora, 'it's not funny.'

'My dears, my darlings, life is funny,' responded Jack, relieved that the visitors were virtually unharmed, but secretly keen to access his sketch pad, to record the recent happenings.

After the air raid the elderly policeman volunteered to walk Catherine to her home, which was conveniently en route to the police station. Catherine shivered as she walked from the house, into the cold night air. 'Wait,' called Dora. She rushed upstairs and came down with a pale blue, rather beautiful, knitted cardigan. 'Wear this home. You've had a shock; you must keep warm.' Catherine took the cardigan gratefully and agreed to drop it back, on her way to work the next day.

'No hurry,' responded Dora.

Madeleine returned home from ARP duty, in the early hours of the morning, looking exhausted. 'Everyone alright here?' she called, as she climbed upstairs.

'Ah there she is, our miniature, but mighty ARP,'

greeted Jack, emerging from the front bedsitting room, dark hair tousled, stripey pyjamas wrinkled and riding up his legs. 'Madge, England's latest defence against Hitler.'

'Long may you remain oblivious to what I've just witnessed tonight,' replied Madeleine, shakily, her face ashen.

'I'll make you a cup of tea,' responded Jack, suddenly realising the state she was in. 'Come back down to the breakfast room.'

The two sat together drinking tea made with powdered milk, Madeleine still in her uniform, minus the tin hat, Jack in his wrinkled pyjamas.

'Tell me all about it,' said Jack gently. 'I can listen.'

'It's not all just about telling people to cover their windows and put lights out you know,' replied Madeleine. 'We patrol in pairs, during and after the raids. We help with first aid if needed and we try to reunite families if they're separated during a raid. And tonight… tonight my partner and I were present where two houses were destroyed, we had to separate a tiny, young child from her dead mother – neither made it to the shelter, but the mother threw herself on top of the child to protect her. The child was covered in her mother's blood and… then we took the child to a centre. She has a grandparent they're going to contact.'

Jack put his hand gently on Madeleine's shoulder. 'You did grand, you helped the child. You're not to blame for this terrible war, we all just have to do whatever we can. Now go and freshen up and get into your bed. I'll send Dora to you.'

CHAPTER 24
HOME OF DREAMS

During one of their war-time visits to Birmingham, William had presented Louis with an old tin, filled with numerous offcuts of leather, wax string and special needles – to repair their shoes and mend or create ingenious styles of handbags, wallets and purses if required. Leather items were rationed so this proved invaluable, as did a supply of simple, hand-drawn diagrams, showing Louis a few easy leather items to begin with. As a young child, he had often watched his father mend their shoes and make simple leather bags for Madeleine, Ida and Joan when they were young children, using offcuts from a local factory.

Louis soon taught himself the skills required and was often to be seen designing and sewing weird and wonderful leather creations – whilst travelling by train or coach each Sunday or in the dressing room, between performances. Eventually many of the people in the show started putting in requests for repairs and for new leather items. Soon all the leather offcuts were used up and he started creating interesting new handbags and purses from tired old ones.

As the war progressed and Birmingham continued to suffer heavy bomb damage, Louis found himself thinking about his father far more than usual and praying that his firm and the family home would not be bombed, or anyone injured. Ultimately his prayers were partially answered, for in the early part of the war, late one evening, whilst Madeleine was on ARP duty, William was reading a favourite history book and Hilda and Annie were tidying the plates away when yet another air raid sounded, shattering the peaceful atmosphere and denying the option of a comfortable night's sleep in a warm bed.

'Annie, Hilda, come to the cellar, bring the gas masks,' ordered William, leading the way and opening the door to the cold, dark dwelling place. Carefully making his way down the uneven concrete steps, using his torch he guided the females safely to chairs. 'Did you close the door properly, Annie?'

'You know I always do,' responded Annie, placing two gas masks on a wooden chair beside her. 'Hilda, where's your gas mask?'

'On the table, beside the blankets and the flasks. I'll make us all some tea,' volunteered Hilda. 'Our poor Madeleine's out in all this. I pray she stays safe.'

'She will,' replied Annie firmly, inwardly hoping she was right. 'William, you're shaking, are you cold?'

'Just a little. I left my second cardigan in the living room.'

'Come and sit by me,' Annie beckoned to the comfortable wide arm of the old armchair.

William walked slowly to the armchair and balanced on the wide, welcoming arm. Annie slipped her hand in his and glanced at his face, in the dimly lit cellar, realising how thin and tired he looked. Hilda passed them a blanket each and the two huddled together for warmth.

The air raid seemed to last longer than usual, with the sound and vibration of bombs penetrating their temporary habitat under the house. At one point the very ground beneath them shook with tremendous force as a crescendo of crashes were heard overhead.

Ultimately, the all clear siren sounded and finally all was peaceful once more as three cold, tired humans made their way carefully up the steep, concrete steps, with William leading the way with his torch once more. He turned the door handle and pushed at the door. Nothing happened.

'Go back down into the cellar,' commanded William. 'The door's stuck. I'm going to have to use a little force.' Turning the handle again and forcing his wiry, but deceptively strong body against the door, he managed to make it move open a couple of inches. As it opened a large piece of wood fell from somewhere above the door and crashed onto the floor. A strong smell of dust, and burning, intertwined with the stench of something revoltingly pungent greeted him. Choking, he tried to see through the small opening. He glimpsed a tangled heap of wood and rubble, where the hallway should be. Gasping for breath and coughing, he walked carefully back down the hard concrete steps.

'We've been hit…' he coughed, 'wood, bricks… door blocked… gas masks on…'

Swiftly Hilda put on her mask, ran up the cellar steps, pushed the door and tried desperately to open it fully. Several small crashes sounded nearby, as the door opened a fraction further, about five inches altogether. Hilda was able to determine the layers of brick, wood and rubble that lay against the door and that indeed the hallway and house no longer stood. They were trapped in the cellar.

'Pa's right. The house is gone…' called Hilda, her voice muffled inside the gas mask. 'We need to keep going up to call for help. Someone's sure to come soon.'

'There's water seeping into the cellar, it's getting higher,' noted Annie, from the depths of her gas mask, offering a series of hand actions to accompany her muffled voice. 'I say we must sit on the steps, near the top and take turns in trying to open the door further and escape.'

'We only tackle the door if no help turns up,' replied William, firmly. 'There's possibly much weight behind the door and if we push it too much it may just burst right through on top of us. It's a miracle it hasn't already.' And so they sat on the final few steps of the cellar, tentatively peering through the gap from time to time and calling out in case anyone was searching the wreckage.

Eventually, after what seemed like days, but was actually only about two hours, they heard a muffled, elderly female voice calling to them. 'Annie, Annie, you there somewhere?'

'I think it's Mary from two doors along,' said Hilda.

'Mary, we're trapped in the cellar, stay away it's not safe,' called Annie, hoping her muffled words could be heard.

'Came in all around me,' called back Mary, her voice wavering a little, 'just left me a hole... to crawl through... at the... top, but...' here the words grew fainter and faded away.

'Mary, stay awake. Are you hurt? Are you wearing a gas mask? Stay awake, we'll all be helped soon,' returned William, in what he hoped was a firm, reassuring tone.

'Oh, dear Lord, I think she's badly injured,' said Annie quietly.

'Listen, Annie, Hilda...' commanded William. 'Hush, both of you, I can hear voices and...'

The sound of heavy footsteps, combined with two or three loud, slightly muffled male voices and a soft female voice, appeared to be drawing near.

'We're trapped!' called William.

'We're in our cellar!' called Annie and Hilda, in unison.

'There's a lady collapsed out there, somewhere. Her name's Mary,' called Annie.

'We have her, she'll be looked after,' came a soft, female reply. 'We've a few things to move before we reach you, but don't you fear, there's a team of three strong Home Guards clearing the way. I'm a nurse. Are any of you hurt?'

'No, we're all unscathed,' reported William.

'If it's safe for you to move down your cellar steps a little, please do so, we need to stabilise what's left of the staircase over your cellar door, before we clear the way for you,' commanded an elderly male voice.

'Will do,' confirmed William.

It took a little over two hours for the rescue team to clear the rubble and secure the area safely to allow Hilda and William and Annie to walk away from their damp, dark prison. All three emerged, holding hands and supporting one another.

'Thank you, thank you, we owe you our lives,' said William, his voice somewhat uneven and his eyes a little moist – perhaps from the dreadful smell of the rubber and strong disinfectant inside his gas mask – perhaps from the thought that there were still volunteers and nurses who cared so much for humanity that they came together, in the most treacherous of conditions, risking their own lives to save others.

'Have you somewhere safe to go? Or shall we walk you to one of the centres for tea and a clean-up?' asked the frailest of the three Home Guards.

'My sister Beatie lives quite nearby,' replied Annie,

'but, our Madeleine's in the ARP and when she returns home to this, she'll think we've…'

'Tell me her surname and we'll get a message through to her, if we can. Then she can meet you at your sister's.'

***

The family lived with Annie's sister Beatie for about four weeks, squashed into her tiny three-bedroomed terraced house. She was wonderfully kind to them and said they could stay as long as they needed, but eventually William found them an elegant, semi-detached four-bedroomed Victorian house to live in, just around the corner from Handsworth Park. 'It belonged to one of the gentlemen in my chess club,' explained William. 'He died a few weeks ago and his daughter wants to sell it, but she's happy to rent it out during the war and if it survives the war, she'll sell it to us at a good price. Now, our Annie, *if* anything happens to me…'

'William, how *dare* you even think such a thing. I'll hear no more of it.'

'You *will* listen,' responded William, standing up and forcing his shoulders back firmly, attempting to assume the stance of a much younger man. 'If anything happens to me, you will still buy it. The money is in the bank in full. The money you've given me to save from your shop each week, savings from my work and money left from the sale of my father's shares in the firm; it's enough to buy that house with no mortgage and never a day's more rent after the war! You know it's all there.

'The children are all doing well. There's no more rainy days to save for. It's our turn now, Annie. It's a good, firm house, number seventy-six, in a road right near the park and there'll always be plenty of room for the young ones to come home to. Space to build new dreams together.'

CHAPTER 25
CALLED TO FIGHT

In 1944, at the age of thirty-three, Louis received his call-up papers – sent, of course, to the new family home in Birmingham – number seventy-six, hence Les Cygne Four returned home to prepare for the inevitable. Initially Louis was a little annoyed as the act was doing particularly well, in a long revue, but eventually his sense of duty won through and he felt proud to serve his country.

'Why haven't I been called up?' voiced Jack, cross at being missed out.

'You're in your forties – perhaps you're too old,' replied Dora gently, 'or perhaps because you are from Southern Ireland?'

'I'm going to join up. I'm as strong as Louis any day. Look at these muscles,' Jack flexed his strong, muscular arms. Unfortunately, following the usual medical examination, Jack was declared *unfit for service* due to a weak heart and advised to lead a calm life.

'My dears, my darlings – *me* lead a calm life. It's not natural, I'd simply die,' Jack's melodramatic voice rang throughout the living room.

'Just as well, you'll be here to carry on with the shows then,' retorted Louis, 'someone has to.'

'You know this house looks more homely, every time we come back,' observed Ida, looking around the living room of number seventy-six. William and Annie, Hilda and Madeleine had been there for more than two years now and little by little they were adding their own particular stamp upon it, with embroidered cushions, crocheted mats and several items salvaged from the wreckage of their old house, including a piano, a wardrobe and dressing table made by Louis in his twenties, a carved dresser and some small incidental odds and ends. Louis' beautiful wooden fort, made for him by his father, was never found and an old album of early photos also perished, but Annie was frequently to be heard saying, 'It's not finery that makes a home, it's people.'

Number seventy-six, as everyone called the new home, was somewhat similar to their previous house, though rather more elegant in terms of the beautiful wide windowsills and very large bay windows. Upon entry, there was a spacious porch, a long, tiled hallway and the usual front parlour and living room, on the right-hand side of the hall, plus a door to a cellar on the left-hand side. The hallway continued and led into a breakfast room, also with a tiled floor. A tiny kitchen, or scullery as it was often called, opened onto to a long, wide garden which overlooked a railway track. An Anderson shelter was cleverly disguised within a mound of grass and rockery plants.

Upstairs, a large front bedroom offered Jack and Dora a spacious bedsitting room and a tiny, square front bedroom provided somewhere for Louis to sleep when needed. A large back bedroom accommodated William and Annie and a long, winding stairway revealed a huge attic room, with sloping ceilings and space for four single beds, wardrobes and dressing tables, a work desk for Madeleine and a sewing area for Hilda.

The house also came with its own resident feline – a large, aged tabby who persisted in jumping in the breakfast room window and sitting on William's lap as he enjoyed a cup of tea beside the coal fire. Assuming the cat to belong to the previous, now deceased house occupant, William adopted him and called him Tiger.

As Louis prepared to go to war, Jack prepared to create a three-handed adagio act. Still under contract for a long tour, he was under pressure to create an act of equal excitement and interest.

'Our Joan is going to be just resting from next week, could you include her, instead of me? She's so very young and glamorous and I'd be glad of a rest for a while,' suggested Dora.

'It wouldn't be Les Cygne Four with two members missing,' responded Louis.

'Then we give it another name,' suggested Ida, 'we create a new, exciting act until you come back from war. Our contract is for our names, not the name of the act and Joan, well we'd add her in, her surname's the same.'

Finally, Joan, Ida and Jack created an attractive and exciting new adagio routine and continued the tour under the name of *The Tania Sisters and Anton*. Joan was also given a solo singing and dancing spot, in the revue, using her normal stage name.

Meanwhile Louis' time to depart leapt upon the family and the goodbyes were not easy. The girls and Annie hugged him, Madeleine gave him a Saint Christopher and Jack patted him on the shoulder and told him to stay alert and healthy. William placed a thin, firm hand on his shoulder, then suddenly gave him a long, fierce hug. 'Do your duty, but don't try to be a hero. We'll not lose another boy. I'm so very, very proud of you, son.'

In 1945 William suffered a stroke. Madeleine was with him when it occurred and insisted on travelling to the hospital, in the ambulance beside him. Within two weeks he was back home, receiving good care and exercising his authority by refusing to learn to walk with a stick. Eventually he progressed to the point where he was even able to walk up and down stairs slowly and could cope with many simple tasks unaided.

Jack, Ida and Joan went back home to visit and felt quite safe in the knowledge that William was being fussed over and cared for competently by Hilda, Dora, their mother and Madeleine. As at their last house they employed a lady to help with some of the washing, but the rest of the household work and cooking was shared by Annie and Hilda. The pair also continued with a little work in Annie's shop and with voluntary war duties – Hilda still doing some cooking at the Emergency Rest Centre and Annie helping the church, but an ongoing routine was established so that William had someone with him at all times. Dora was always around to entertain with piano and dance, make cups of tea and read with him. Then Madeleine would return from the office each evening to sit beside him and play chess or chat quietly.

Meanwhile, life in the army was a cultural shock for Louis, but he coped well. He was used to mixing with all types of people and enjoyed the comradeship, but following orders, well that wasn't so easy. Ultimately, however, he did his duty, served his country and survived the war, rejoicing when it ended in May 1945. Eagerly he awaited his official date of freedom or demobilisation (demob) – longing to be with his family once more, keen to be beside his father again, to see for himself how he was coping after his stroke, perhaps even to have a game of chess or draughts with him, if he was still able to play.

In September 1945 Louis' long-awaited demob descended upon him. Having asked Hilda to go into his little room and find one of his favourite Savile Row suits, he had requested her to post it to a guest house near the railway station, not far from his barracks, hence on his first day of freedom from the army, he wore his demob suit – provided for all soldiers leaving World War Two service – made his way to the guest house, thanked and tipped the proprietor and asked if he could use a room to change in. He put on his favourite suit and good leather shoes, lovingly folded the double-breasted demob suit, complete with waistcoat, hoping his father, who only had two good suits and always refused offers of a new one, would like it. It was unpretentious, free and yet reasonably smart, hence his father may enjoy wearing it. Their height was similar and though his father had grown thinner in recent years, Hilda would be able to tailor it to fit stylishly.

After an extremely long train journey, a seemingly endless bus ride and a short walk Louis stood before the front gate of number seventy-six, glancing at the impressive front garden as he eagerly walked the last few steps to the front door, his heart almost singing with the pleasure of being home – seeing his family again. Hilda opened the door, before he could put his key in the lock or even reach for the brass door knocker.

'Hilda, it's so good to be...' Louis stopped, suddenly noticing Hilda's white face.

'Whatever's wrong? Why is the house so quiet? Tell me, what's...'

'Come into the parlour.'

Louis' heart leapt with fear as Hilda beckoned silently, indicating he should sit down with her.

'What's happened?' Louis responded, his voice edged with fear.

'Louis, our pa passed yesterday.'

'But... but... he was getting better. How, how...'

'Mama went to wake him after his afternoon nap and he'd passed in his sleep. Doctor said he possibly had another stroke while he slept.'

'And *no one* had the decency to let me know yesterday?' Louis' voice rose in anger. 'You all *knew* and you let me travel home expecting to see my father. Why? Why?'

'Everyone was in shock. Mama said best we told you, not your commanding officer.'

'Ludicrous, I should have been told,' shouted Louis. 'How dare you keep it from me?'

Hilda put her arms around him. 'Don't be vexed, our Louis, Mama wanted me to tell you. She was worried you'd be in a state travelling home knowing what had happened. It was a shock to us all. He was doing so well we all thought...' Hilda's voice trembled momentarily. Taking a deep calming breath she continued, 'Jack, Dora and Joan arrived the day before yesterday, ready to see you. They're here for a week. Not sure who's covering their act. Don't think they cared, just wanted to welcome you home so...'

'So where is everyone?' said Louis, his voice still edged with anger.

'In the living room. Now lower your voice, gather your thoughts and don't be angry anymore. Mama needs us all to be strong.'

Hilda walked behind Louis as he made his way into the living room. Everyone was sitting silently. Madeleine and Joan were holding books, but neither seemed absorbed by the contents, Dora held embroidery and Ida clutched her crochet work, neither were engrossed in their tasks. Annie sat at the table, pouring tea for everyone, her face seemed suddenly old, lined with sorrow, almost but not quite beaten.

As Louis entered the room Annie held out her arms. 'I'm so sorry, son.'

'It's not your fault,' responded Louis, his anger replaced with compassion. 'You looked after our father – our pa – you've always been there for him. The very best wife he could ever have wished for.'

'Sit down, drink some tea, we must all be strong,' Annie spoke firmly, but kindly, struggling to stay in control of her emotions. 'We have much to plan and organise, your father would want us to be strong.'

Louis sat down and a large, elderly tabby cat strolled into the room, jumped onto his lap and proceeded to wash itself.

'Get down, Tiger,' he growled, pushing the cat down. 'Not on my best suit.'

'He always sat on our pa's lap,' commented Hilda, 'think he likes men.'

'Oh come on then, if you must,' responded Louis, picking the cat up and making a fuss of it.

For Les Cygne Four and for the whole family, 1945 had ended with sorrow, but also fresh hope for the world was at peace once more. Annie encouraged everyone to gather around the piano again for she said their father would be happy to know they were still singing and dancing.

William
Taken by a family
member in the
1940s.

PART 4
FINAL YEARS 1945–1955

CHAPTER 26
IN SEARCH OF
A MISSING GLOVE

In November 1945, Joan, Ida and Jack performed as The Tania Sisters and Anton for the very last time and Les Cygne Four found themselves united *on the boards* once more, touring Yorkshire and Scotland and then moving on to Cheltenham Opera House for the pantomime season in *Aladdin*. This left Joan free to focus on her solo routine, though not for long, for in 1946 she was to leave England for good. Having fallen head over heels in love with a tall, good looking American soldier, she was soon to become a GI bride and seek her fortune in Texas. Joan's petite figure looked totally swamped beside her six-foot GI, but he seemed to treat her with much kindness and respect. Needless to say her future plans were the subject of much discussion amidst Les Cygne Four.

'Mama was afraid Joan may be too in love and too young to know her own mind,' remarked Dora, 'but she's in her twenties now and besides, when has our Joan ever not known her own mind?'

'She walked right out of school at the age of five,' remarked Louis, 'went along to the school two streets away and asked if she could go there instead, because one of the nuns at her school was always cross with her.'

'I remember,' contributed Ida. 'Our mama was livid

when the headmistress sent a note home, offering Joan a place. It wasn't even a Catholic school.'

'I remember Hilda telling me about it,' said Dora. 'Mama went down to the school and asked to be shown round. She agreed for Joan to go there as long as she could take in her book of saints.'

'Joan loved it there. They really encouraged her with her studies,' remarked Louis. 'Our Joan will be fine wherever she goes. If she doesn't like Texas, she'll soon find her way home to Birmingham.'

Standing by her plan, to marry her GI and to live in Texas, Joan – as always – made the right decision. Within a few years she had opened her own dance and drama studio and had a beautiful young daughter. Between her duties as a wife and mother and the running of her studio, she helped her husband with his business and the pair of them ran a Summer Camp each year, approved by their daughter who enjoyed exploring all the fun activities.

Having played in several revues and pantomimes with Joan from time to time, Les Cygne Four had really missed her when she finally went to Texas. And so, when Madeleine asked if she could spend three weeks' holiday touring with them, they welcomed the idea with open arms, keen to show her a little of their world at last.

Now the proud owners of a 1931 Packard, Les Cygne Four were able to offer Madeleine a very comfortable ride, with plenty of room for her travel bags and several spare pairs of shoes. Madeleine liked shoes. She purchased new pairs to match many of her outfits. With her very small shoe size it was often necessary to have them specially handmade, but this didn't deter her. With most things she was not extravagant, but with shoes, well it was different – just a minor weakness…

The first part of the tour involved a long trip from Birmingham down to Eastbourne. The weather was glorious when they set out fairly early on the Sunday and the five of them were making such good progress that they stopped for a mini picnic and flasks of tea along the way and then again for tea and scones in a little country café as they drew towards Sussex, with Madeleine delighting in a place at the front, on the luxurious wide seat between Jack and Louis, when they clambered back into the car for the final lap of the journey.

Unfortunately, it was that final lap of the journey that proved to be troublesome, for as they reached the remaining twenty-five miles or so they found themselves travelling towards dark clouds and the promise of extremely wild weather amidst the Sussex countryside. Soon that promise became reality as torrential rain descended in a fierce sheet and the Packard's windscreen wipers struggled to cope with the level of rain forced upon them. Thunder roared and the land went suddenly rather dark. As Louis steered the car around narrow lanes, through horrendously hilly countryside, the wind causing the trees, along the edge of the road, to beat maliciously upon the sides of the car, the only light was provided by the Packard's headlights and the fairly frequent flashes of forked lightning.

'Pull this car over,' demanded Jack. 'Are you trying to kill us all?'

'You know my thoughts on that,' responded Louis. 'I'll not stop until we're at the digs. We've been through worse than this.'

'I'm not so sure about that,' contributed Dora. 'But

you're right we must go on.'

'Then our public will be disappointed for there'll be no Cygnes left to entertain them,' replied Jack in his melodramatic fashion.

'Stop your foolish talk, Jack,' commanded Madeleine, in her most business-like tone. 'Our Louis could drive this car safely through the ocean if he had to.'

'Well, I say we keep quiet and let him concentrate on steering us all to safety,' advised Ida.

For a while the journey continued with no further human interaction and Louis was left in peace to do his best to guide them through the storm. As he reached an incline, in semi darkness, the road narrowed and the darkness increased. Suddenly crosswinds, delighting in an unexpected absence of roadside trees, flung their full force upon the brave Packard, momentarily taking Louis by surprise. That moment was all that was needed. Louis lost control of the car as it careered off the road and down a slippery hillside.

'Hold on to something, put your heads low on your knees,' shouted Louis, as the car raced down the slippery slope and he attempted to slow it down. A sudden flash of lightning offered an unwelcome view of a wide brick wall at the base of the hill.

'I love you, Dora, keep your head down, hold on,' called Jack suddenly, gripping the seat, his knuckles white. 'Madge, head down.'

As the strong Packard met the wide brick wall the sound was tremendous, puncturing and triumphing over the background rumble of nature's stormy elements. The three sisters screamed. The men were silent for a few seconds. Then Jack moaned gently to himself and Louis, who had slipped beneath the steering wheel, tentatively tested his limbs to see if he could still move. Slowly he slid back into his seat, bruised but virtually unscathed.

Dora and Ida had been flung across the back seat and were now in each other's arms, thankful to have survived.

'Praise the Lord we're all alive,' exclaimed Jack. 'All alive... where's Madeleine... Madge...'

'I'm down here, at your feet,' called Madeleine. 'Just emerging now. I'm only bruised.'

'Slowly, Madeleine, take my hand,' responded Louis as he leant forward to help her back onto her seat.

'Thank heavens the brakes are good on this,' observed Louis. 'I'd almost managed to stop it before it hit the wall. Things would have been worse if...'

'Are you hurt? How many of you are there?' called a strong male voice belonging to a short, rather wide gentleman, in his mid-forties, pushing through the wild wind and rain and slowly winding his way towards them, shining a large torch. The gentleman, copiously wrapped in a huge windcheater, was followed by a female, of similar short, but generous proportions, in identical apparel, also shining a large torch.

Louis opened the car door and stepped out to greet them. The heavy metal door was almost whipped from his hands, by the wind, as he struggled to close it. Holding fast to the door handle, lest the wind whisk him away forever, he greeted the couple. 'Is this your wall? Naturally we'll pay for any damage.'

'Oh, don't you worry about that,' responded the gentleman. 'It's still in one piece. Are *you* alright?'

'All a bit bruised, but nothing serious.'

'Let's get you all up to the house for a cup of tea or something stronger. Then we can arrange some lads to push the car back up onto the road.'

Slowly, Les Cygne Four and Madeleine followed the couple several yards to a wrought iron gate, set in the very wall they had crashed into, then along a narrow winding pathway to a large semi-detached cottage, with a roaring log fire.

'I'm George and this is my wife, Jane. Now shall we get you tea or would you like something stronger? Brandy? Sherry?'

'Tea would be grand,' replied Jack.

'You know you're very lucky,' remarked Jane. 'Two weeks ago, a young couple died when their car hit that very same wall, a little further along, just outside our son's cottage it was. Going at a speed they were and in a smallish car.'

'Only put the wall up to keep the farmer's sheep out. It stops them coming into our gardens,' remarked George.

As they sipped tea and exchanged pleasantries with Jane, George and his son, from the cottage next door, organised a team of local men to push the Packard back up the slippery slope and onto the narrow road once more. The men refused all mention of money for their help and cheerfully waved Madeleine and Les Cygne Four on their way.

Luckily the Packard, whilst scratched, slightly dented and extremely muddy, still worked and they were able to continue their journey. The weather remained quite wild, but the journey had to continue. Louis refused to be beaten. They must reach their digs.

After driving for about half an hour, Louis started to relax a little, they seemed to be driving away from the dreadful weather. The atmosphere within the car was peaceful – well for a short while…

'Stop, stop the car,' demanded Ida, with a distinct air of authority in her voice.

'Whatever for?' queried Louis.

'I've lost a glove. My new white gloves. I had them in my hands as we got out of the car and went to the cottage for tea. You'll have to drive back.'

'You very nearly lost your life and now you want me to go back for a lost glove,' growled Louis. 'Just buy some more.'

'It's madness, darlings, madness. We'll not survive a second back there,' contributed Jack.

Louis meanwhile sent forth a fierce paroxysm of heated sentences to Ida as she continued to demand to return to the scene of their accident.

Ida dismissed the outburst with a shrug of her shoulders. 'Very well, stop the car. I shall walk back. I'll not be done out of my best pair of gloves. What'll I do with just one?'

Louis, sorely tempted to tell her what to do with the remaining glove, slowed the car down and pulled up at the side of the road.

'You're never going to let her walk,' responded Madeleine. 'Surely not.'

'No,' retorted Louis angrily, 'but I've to pull over to work out how to safely turn this car around on such a narrow stretch.'

Finally, driving back towards the scene of the accident, everyone was silent except Jack who uttered, 'We're going forth to meet our maker. All for a glove.'

Arriving back at the scene of their earlier miraculous escape, Louis steered the car skilfully along the narrow road, gradually to a halt, as far from the edge of the hillside as possible. Thankfully the weather had settled a little, though it was still raining fairly hard. He and Jack climbed out, Louis stepping into a mass of slimy mud, beside the road and Jack stepping into a deep puddle. Using a torch they made their way carefully down the slippery hillside, entering George and Jane's garden as quietly as possible and scouring the ground for the glove. There was no sign of it. Surreptitiously they exited the garden, closed the gate as quietly as possible and climbed the hillside once more.

'Well, that's it, she's lost it,' remarked Louis.

'We tried,' contributed Jack. 'Now let's get to the digs.'

'No more delays,' agreed Louis, as they approached the car once more. Shining his torch along the side of the car, to enable Jack to climb in safely, he spotted something white and suspiciously familiar, fluttering on the ribbed running board, caught on part of the metal trim, beside Ida's door. Snatching it up – half in anger, half in wonder – he climbed into the car, leaned over towards the back seat and threw the glove towards Ida. 'Next time you demand that we retrace a journey, in treacherous weather conditions, in search of a missing glove, be sure to look on the running board first.'

'However did…' gasped Ida. 'It was windy. It…'

'Caught on the metal strip,' responded Louis, 'flapping around in the wind.'

Ida adorned a humorous expression of mock mournfulness, partially hiding her face behind her hands.

'It's not funny,' growled Louis.

'It is,' laughed Dora. 'Shall I be first to smother her with a cushion?' Dora picked up one of several loose cushions adorning the back seat.

Louis struggled hard not to smile, but eventually he had to agree it was vaguely funny, travelling miles in search of a glove that was with them on the running board all along – chance in a million really.

CHAPTER 27
WOOLLY COATS
AND ROGUE RATS

Although in the forties and fifties, some theatres were in need of fresh paint, had tatty, sometimes almost threadbare velvet seats and worn, faded curtains, the magic was still present. As the music played and the curtain rose, audiences were captivated once more – whisked away to the wonderful world of make believe, lured into the enchanting ambience of pantomime or simply hypnotised within the dazzle, the music, the dance and the eclectic skills displayed within each variety show or spectacular revue. Spellbound, their lives were enriched by each transient performance.

Les Cygne Four had enjoyed being involved in some spectacular revues and pantomimes as with a colourful production involving Tommy Lorne and Elkan Simons, where Les Cygne Four were cast as slaves dancing to entertain the king. In the same show there was a scene involving a crescent moon that moved gracefully as a girl sat upon it singing. It was an ingenious contraption, and no one could understand how it worked. In another show, involving a magnificent underwater scene, a large oyster shell opened and Ida stepped out, to join the others in their adagio dance.

Creativity and originality were key to a successful show, but sometimes Les Cygnes Four found ingenious ideas could be hard to follow through successfully, as with the idea of using live sheep at the Metropolitan in Edgeware Road, for a production of *Little Bo Peep*. Les Cygnes Four were, of course, performing their usual adagio routine, but as with most pantomimes they were required to play various characters, if needed.

At one point Louis, all five-foot-four of him, was asked to lead three live sheep across the stage, say a few words and then lead them off into the wings. A simple task some may assume, but sheep are unique, they do not think like humans, hence – during full dress rehearsal – when Louis started to lead three large, extremely well fed, marginally confused woolly creatures towards centre stage, ready to utter his few words, the leading sheep decided to bolt straight into the wings. Naturally – being sheep – the other two followed, sending Louis flying face down onto the stage. Still attached to their ropes, he slithered after them, still face down, off into the wings amidst much laughter from fellow thespians.

True to theatrical tradition, however, a bad rehearsal led to a good opening night. The sheep were reasonably well-behaved, though a bucket and disinfectant was required in the wings, to clear up a little mess as one sheep had been rather nervous and Louis did exit the stage somewhat faster than intended, with just enough time to say his few words, before flying off into the wings led by his three woolly creatures.

As television became more popular and affordable, audiences started to grow smaller and some theatres closed totally. Over the years others became bingo halls and other businesses, hence good theatrical bookings were not always as easy to obtain. On one occasion Les Cygne Four were engaged at a sad, extremely washed-out theatre, one they had never played before and – as it turned out – never wished to play again.

'Whatever have we come to?' asked Ida as they

walked towards their dressing room, trying hard not to brush against the damp walls, complete with dramatically peeling paintwork. The smell of the corridor was atrocious, a rare combination of urine and rat poison.

'If this is the best we're offered, it's time to leave the business,' exclaimed Louis. 'Did you not know what this place was like?'

Jack shook his head, 'I've heard a few tales, but it's part of the tour. Couldn't refuse it. The audience still matters. Give it your best effort.'

'That's if anyone ever sets foot in the place. It feels dead,' growled Louis.

As they entered the dressing room, the smell of damp, intertwined with a musty, dusty aroma enveloped them.

'Well, it's only for a week. I say we must make the best of it,' advised Ida, attempting a cheerful smile, as a gentle knock sounded on their dressing room door.

Louis opened the door to two dancers who were part of the show. 'Yes, is something wrong?'

'Two dead rats in the dressing room,' gasped the tallest of the two girls.

'Don't worry, you shall share with us for now,' responded Dora. 'The boys can go in the corridor or turn their backs while you change. Bring your things in. You can report the rats after the show.'

'Oh, my dears, my darlings – what have we come to?' exclaimed Jack.

'I thought you said we must give it our best,' growled Louis.

'And so you must,' responded Jack. 'It's part of the tour and every audience matters, but...'

'Well, let's look at it this way. Things can only get

better,' said Ida laughing, but she was soon to discover how wrong she was, for as they stepped onto the stage it was obvious the theatre was dying. It was less than a quarter full, but the audience were extremely appreciative and responsive, gasping and clapping in all the correct places, there were just not enough of them. Returning to their digs, they were greeted with the familiar smell of boiled cabbage, no milk for tea and an absence of hot water, hence had to ask to boil kettles in order to wash.

The next evening, as they entered the dressing room Ida and Dora shrieked in horror as they observed a rat virtually hanging onto the trouser leg of Louis' neatly hung costume, plus a mass of rat droppings under a wooden chair and nibble marks along the waist of Jack's costume. Luckily Ida and Dora had hung their costumes on hangers, from a high hook, hence they were undamaged.

'We've been to some bad bookings before, but this beats them all,' groaned Louis.

'Never in all my days have I seen such dirt and squaller,' agreed Jack. 'We'll not wear those costumes until they've had some disinfectant on them. We'll all be having diseases.'

Dora produced a glass bottle of brown, strong smelling Dettol from the bag of supplies they carried around. 'Here, will this do?'

Ida, meanwhile, searched in her bag for some perfume. 'I'll not be thrown around by someone smelling of that dreadful stuff, dab a little perfume on top.'

'And I'll not walk around smelling of ladies perfume,' exclaimed Louis. Eventually he found some aftershave and dabbed it on the offending items.

That evening, after the show, they all hung their costumes up as high as possible, thus making it harder for the rats to nibble them. The week seemed to go by very slowly, but eventually it drew to an end and Les Cygne Four were delighted to escape their week of horror, vowing never to perform there again.

CHAPTER 28
JUST RESTING

Les Cygne Four had been fortunate not to have much time just resting, having managed to attract work – often very long contracts – throughout most of their years in the theatre, but twice in the early 1950s they found themselves at the end of a good tour with nothing to move on to. On the first occasion, their final show was in London, hence Louis and Jack visited their agent plus most London variety agents, but there did not seem to be anything. Travelling around various theatrical haunts looking for work, it was usual to meet other acts, many of whom they had worked with in the past. Exchanging words each would ask, 'Where are you playing?' Jack and Louis would reply, 'Just resting. What are *you* up to now?'

'Just resting, heaven knows for how long,' or, 'Just resting, something's bound to turn up soon,' would often be the standard replies received.

Just as Louis and Jack were about to head back to their digs and prepare to return to Birmingham, a friendly pianist, whom they'd worked with on several occasions, suggested they try the place he'd just come from. 'They didn't want me. I was sent for an audition, but a younger pianist came out all smiles and they're going to *let me know*. We all know what *that* means. They're still looking for a speciality act though. Hurry on over there, you may be lucky.'

Louis and Jack rushed to the given address. Happily, this resulted in a long contract – based on their successful performance in a previous revue.

They returned to the digs triumphant. Sometimes it was just a case of knowing the right person and being in the right place at the right time.

Another time, following a long tour, Les Cygne Four returned to Birmingham *just resting*. The first couple of days home seemed a novelty, it was wonderful to relax in comparative comfort, enjoy good food and be fussed over by their mother and Hilda, plus catch up with Madeleine, but pretty soon they started to feel as though they were stagnating. Each day they listened eagerly for a phone call or a telegram from their agent with news of the next show, but to no avail.

'Oh well, I suppose something will turn up,' said Louis, on the eighth morning, attempting to convince himself, Jack, Dora and Ida, whilst wistfully observing the telephone in the hallway, willing it to ring.

'We've only been out a week,' responded Jack, 'but we may already be forgotten. It takes but the blink of an eye. One day topping the bill, the next in the gutter.'

'Oh, go on out, go play a game of tennis the pair of you,' ordered Ida impatiently.

'We've had some good work and a rest won't do any of us any harm,' contributed Dora. 'We'll do some practice tomorrow. Hire a studio from Madame Lehmiski's.'

'Perhaps we should just give it all up and find something else to do,' suggested Louis. 'If nothing turns up soon, as Jack says they'll forget in the blink of an eye, so we'll be finished anyway.'

'Oh, for goodness' sake go away and have that game of tennis,' repeated Ida, 'we'll listen in for the phone or a telegram.'

'And if you see us dancing all the way to the tennis

courts, you'll know we're in luck,' added Dora, giving a little twirl and taking Ida on a sudden waltz along the hallway, her blue eyes sparkling with laughter.

Annie came bustling from the breakfast room, in her usual determined manner, swiftly followed by the latest addition to her family, a reddish-brown Pekingese dog – Kim – bouncing at her heels. Observing Ida at forty-one and Dora ten years her senior, waltzing along the stone hallway. She smiled. 'Never lose that spirit, it will stand you in good stead whatever befalls you both in life.'

As Dora steered Ida around and the two proceeded to waltz in the opposite direction Kim decided it was time to participate, she followed them yapping and snapping at their heels as they danced their way back into the living room and flopped onto the little sofa laughing. Meanwhile Jack and Louis, now dressed for tennis – rackets in their hands – escaped through the front door and made their way to Handsworth Park.

After three weeks and still no work transpiring, everyone was feeling down and planning for the possibility of no more bookings. Jack and Louis spoke of opening a guest house somewhere by the sea.

'Who'd cook for the guests?' queried Dora.

'Well, certainly not you or Ida, they'd never survive,' replied Louis. 'And our Hilda's settled here with her dressmaking and she still works in Mama's shop, so you'll not persuade her to leave Birmingham.'

'You can cook a bit,' remarked Ida, 'you could learn a bit more.'

'You'll not get me running around cooking,' retorted Louis.

'We'd pay someone to do the evening meals and I'd do the breakfasts,' responded Jack.

Louis looked doubtful. 'I'm not really for this guest house lark. Perhaps for you and Dora maybe, but I know I might want to marry one day and have children.'

'If you find a girl who lives up to your expectations,' laughed Ida.

'I can't help having high standards. I enjoy their company for a few weeks and then I'm bored with them. Aggie was the only girl I thought perhaps I may fall in love with.'

Ida was silent, Aggie had lived in London during the war and Louis had lost contact with her following heavy bombing in the blitz. Her house was no longer there and he'd no way of knowing if she'd survived. Naturally he'd dated many theatrical females since then and sometimes they parted when a tour ended, but mostly he drifted away from each one within a few short weeks.

'You know, Jack, you could be a manager or agent, you've lived and breathed the business for so many years. Our Louis could too,' suggested Ida.

'My dears, variety's dying – my darlings, they'll be no one left to manage soon,' responded Jack.

'You've a business diploma, Louis,' reminded Dora. 'Remember Mama made you do one evening a week, when you finished your cabinet making apprenticeship – just in case it was needed.'

'Not sure it's worth much,' remarked Louis. 'Mostly arithmetic and paperwork. I'd rather start a small cabinet making business, if the need's there. I'd not survive sitting in an office all day. Jack knows what I mean.'

'I could no more go back to office work than fly to the moon,' agreed Jack.

'You've a degree from Dublin University. Could you teach?' asked Dora.

'Me teach? I'd tell them all to go and live their young lives, not sit around in dusty lecture rooms,' responded Jack. 'What about the guest house idea? Dora? Anyone?'

Happily, within an hour or so of this rather depressing conversation, a telegram arrived. All four of them rushed eagerly to the door to greet the poor young delivery gentleman. Seeing the wild gleam in their eyes as they viewed the envelope in his hand, he promptly passed it to Louis, backed away a little and then rushed down the path, leapt back onto his small motorcycle and sped along the road as hastily as possible.

Meanwhile Ida, Dora and Jack gathered around Louis, in the porch, as he held the precious envelope.

'Open it, our Louis, come on...' demanded Ida eagerly.

'In the living room,' ordered Louis. 'Not in the porch.'

Obediently they followed him into the living room. As they sat down he started to fumble and tear at the envelope in an excited manner.

'They'll be nothing left of it soon,' remarked Dora.

Finally drawing the paper from the envelope Louis read aloud: '*Can offer show. Phone...*' Dora rushed for the phone and gave it to Louis.

'Hope we get it,' gasped Ida.

'May need to audition,' remarked Dora as Louis finished an extremely short conversation on the phone.

'We've got it, subject to the usual conditions,' he shouted triumphantly. 'Long tour – Moss Empires – top cast. Rehearsals start in two weeks.'

A cacophony of excited chatter burst forth from the living room. Annie and Hilda came rushing along the hallway – Annie a little breathless as she attempted to keep up with Hilda.

'Whatever's all this commotion?'

'We're going back on tour,' said Dora, rushing to hug her mother in excitement.

'Perhaps the house will be peaceful again,' replied Annie smiling, secretly wishing that the house would remain lively and chaotic forever.

CHAPTER 29
ON TOP OF THE WORLD &
SMITTEN FOR LIFE

In spite of their time spent *just resting* – in the early 1950s, plus the continued slow decline of variety – in April 1952 theatre life was going with a swing for Les Cygne Four with a steady flow of work coming in. They were able to send some money back to the family in Birmingham once more though their mother insisted it was not needed. Now seventy-four, she no longer ran her little shop, but Hilda and Madeleine both worked hard and paid their way. Eventually Louis and Jack arranged to buy the lease on the house for Annie, so that the property and land became freehold with no further need for her to pay a small annual fee to the landowner. They also insisted that she use some money to visit Joan in America, for Annie had yet to meet her first grandchild.

With rehearsals for an eight-month revue about to begin in London and the verbal promise of a six-month variety tour straight after, they had one full day left for relaxation. Ida and Dora planned to treat themselves to some attractive new daytime clothes and Louis and Jack insisted on going to Savile Row for some new shirts.

'I don't know why you boys want Savile Row. I remember when our Hilda made all your shirts,' remarked Ida.

'And excellent they were too,' agreed Louis, 'but she's not in London and Savile Row is.'

'There *are* other places.'

'But the gentlemen listen when I ask them to make

wide collars and they've a wonderful selection of colours to choose from. You know how much I hate white shirts.'

'Pity we're not playing Brighton,' contributed Jack, 'there's that little antique shop Dora and I like.' Collecting small antiques, to display in their bedsitting room in Birmingham, had become almost an obsession with Jack and Dora.

'Well, I say it's a good thing,' retorted Ida, 'I'm loath to unpack any day clothes lately, for fear of coming across some new piece of china on its way to Birmingham. I swear I'll end up breaking one of them one of these days.'

After a pleasurable few hours shopping, Les Cygne Four opted for an early night, in preparation for a long rehearsal the next day, for over and above their minor materialistic pursuits they continued to live and breathe theatre, rejoicing in each new tour. Spellbound and nervous, every time they heard the opening bars of their music, they delighted in their ability to captivate an audience after so many years.

Entering the large rehearsal room, the next day, Louis experienced a mystical almost intuitive awareness that something important was going to happen that day. Swiftly the moment was lost amidst the hustle and bustle of rehearsal and everything continued like clockwork, including the usual minor mistakes and interruptions that frequently occurred during a first rehearsal and indeed – on a smaller scale – throughout most rehearsals.

It was during Les Cygne Four's final routine that something wonderful, magical and unexpected occurred. As Louis caught Ida and Jack spun Dora, miraculously rotating her into a final artistic position, Louis noticed a young brunette standing – across the room – observing. Their eyes met and that was the beginning of a whole new chapter in Louis' life. For within that split second he felt the presence of a beautiful female spirit just waiting to be discovered and as all the remaining acts came together – for a final picturesque musical scene – he knew that somehow he must find an opportunity to speak with her. Luckily this presented itself as the rehearsal ended and the various individuals and acts drifted apart.

'Where are you off to, our Louis?' asked Ida, as Louis spied the young brunette and started to march away from Les Cygne Four.

'Never you mind,' retorted Louis, 'I'll not be long.'

Walking briskly towards the young lady, he introduced himself. 'I'm Louis Cygne, I noticed you watching the act. I hope you don't mind me asking, but did you like it? And may I ask your name?'

'It's Veronica, but people call me Vee or Vera,' she responded shyly, in a beautiful Surrey accent. 'Yes, I was watching the act. I thought it very skilled and rather exciting.'

'Thank you. I'm glad you liked it. Oh, do you like poetry?' Louis noticed a book of Tennyson in the outer pocket of the cream leather vanity bag beside Vera.

'I adore it and I love music and painting.'

'I like Shakespeare. Do you like his sonnets?'

'Some, but not all.'

'I heard you sing during rehearsal. You have a beautiful voice.'

'Thank you.'

'Are your family musical like you?'

'Mother plays the piano, Dad plays the violin and they both sing in a philharmonic choir.'

And so the conversation continued for a little while. Just chatting about poetry and music and simple things. He didn't plunge straight in and ask her out, but gradually, as the revue progressed and toured from London to various towns and cities, they were drawn together.

When they reached City Varieties Leeds, in West Yorkshire, Vera was fascinated by its size. It was really quite small compared with many theatres and music halls. She wondered how Les Cygne Four would complete their routine safely. Luckily they had played it many times and were used to making minor adaptations to their routine, one being that often, in a final throw involving Ida, instead of being caught by Louis, she was deliberately thrown over the backcloth, disappeared from view, landed on soft mattresses provided specially and then appeared from the wings, jumping into Louis' arms, for the final pose. The audience would gasp as she disappeared and cheer and clap as she reappeared.

When eventually the revue reached Bath in Somerset, Louis and Vera were often to be found, between rehearsals and shows, in a boat together rowing along the river and chatting about their families. Ida, Jack and Dora often shared a boat and then met up with Vera and Louis in a little tea shop nearby.

'My eldest brother was a Marine Commando during the war,' volunteered Vera, in answer to a question from Louis one day, whilst boating. 'My other brother was in the Navy and my sister was a leading Wren. I was still at school when the war ended. How old were you?'

'When it ended?' Louis panicked, in that moment suddenly realising the age difference between them. Until that minute, he simply hadn't considered it. 'I was, well – over thirty.'

Vera gasped, 'I, I didn't realise. You look so young and so do your sisters.'

'I'm sorry, I didn't mean to let you think otherwise. I… Shall I walk you back to your digs?'

'Don't be silly, it's a beautiful afternoon. I, I just didn't think you were so much older than me. Shall I take a turn rowing?'

'If you don't row round in endless small circles like yesterday,' responded Louis with a grin.

'I'll push you overboard in a minute,' laughed Vera. 'Shall we sing as we row?'

'Why not, though I warn you my voice isn't trained like yours. Where did you train?'

'A school of music and drama, five evenings a week, in London. Then because I passed all my music exams quite young, I was put forward for a free scholarship to a music college, but, I – well, I kept going to auditions until I got into show business instead.'

'Why ever did you do that with your beautiful soprano voice?'

Vera smiled, her eyes alive with the joy of life, 'Excitement, adventure. First, I was in a show as a kangaroo in *Robinson Crusoe*, then I was head girl with the Marietta Dancers – I still dance with them sometimes – Marietta's a wonderful person – but I'm mostly singing solo now. I adore classical music, but I love to sing most everyday songs – just as a mezzo. Shall we sing 'Mona Lisa'?'

'I'll take the oars again first. I've seen the way you

move your arms as you sing. I'll not risk losing both oars, not even for Nat King Cole.'

Vera laughed. Soon her clear, powerful voice rang out across the river, complemented by Louis' deep baritone, causing several boaters to turn their heads towards the music. Jack, Ida and Dora – sharing a boat – looked rather worried.

'My dears, my darlings, he's smitten. I know it,' uttered Jack. 'He hasn't sung off key yet. He *always* goes off key. She's worked her magic upon him.'

'He's even bought a book of Tennyson and he's learning bits by heart,' added Dora. 'I heard him reciting it when I was going across the landing the other night.'

'Don't be silly, he'll never be smitten. He likes his freedom too much,' responded Ida.

Meanwhile, Louis looked across at Vera as she sang and asked himself an age-old question, the question he always asked, whenever he had been dating a lady for a few weeks: *Could I wake up to that face and that voice, that personality, every morning?* Suddenly, instead of the usual clear-cut *No,* he was certain that he wanted to see Vera's face, hear her voice and experience her beautiful personality every day for the rest of his life.

Vera – taken by a family member in the 1950s

CHAPTER 30
A BRAVE SPIRIT DEPARTS

As 1953 crept into existence, with a fierce deluge of theatres to play and the usual hectic routine of travel, rehearsals and shows each week, Dora slowly felt her body begin to falter. She could not point to any one, specific problem at first and just thought perhaps age was beginning to catch up with her. Her eyes still danced with light and laughter. Her spirit still embraced a love of life – the need to dance, run wild, swim, ride horses, travel and experience life to the full, but when her spirit said run, her body felt drained.

As their tour progressed Dora found herself longing for a few days' holiday, back home in Birmingham, just a chance to catch up and feel strong again. Their present contract was due to end in March, but that was six weeks away and Dora was beginning to have a sneaky feeling that she was in fact quite ill. Her limbs felt bruised after each performance, she was often out of breath and coughed a fair bit, but the scariest thing she'd noticed was a tenderness in one side of her breast. It all seemed to have gradually taken over, amidst her usual whirl of activity.

Just four weeks from the end of the tour Dora spoke with Jack one morning in their digs. 'I've to see a doctor, as soon as I can. I think I need a tonic – something to give me energy.'

'Let me see your beautiful face,' responded Jack, concerned, as he sat beside her on the double bed and gently cupped her face within his hands. 'You look tired, perhaps ill. Darling, tell me what's wrong. It's not just a tonic needed, is it?'

'I've. Well, I think…' started Dora, suddenly pausing not quite sure what to mention first.

'Tell me anything. I love you. You can't shock me.'

Dora shared all her symptoms quickly and calmly.

'You shall have the very best doctor right now.' Jack marched down to the kitchen where Mrs D. the landlady was busy preparing breakfast. Asking for the big telephone book and permission to use her phone, he telephoned a prominent local doctor.

'He'll be very expensive. We've the free National Health Service now you know,' contributed Mrs D.

'And that's grand,' responded Jack, 'but I need my wife to see an expert straight away.'

Hurriedly Louis was summoned to drive Dora to the doctor. After giving Dora a full examination, he took Jack to one side and expressed his concern. 'I'm very much afraid it may be breast cancer, but I would like her to see a specialist friend of mine this afternoon. He's an expert and can examine her further.'

Shaking almost uncontrollably Jack grasped the doctor's lapel, 'Can she be treated?'

'Wait to see my colleague. He's the expert.'

Ultimately, after seeing no less than three private specialists, within five days, it was confirmed that Dora had breast cancer that had possibly spread to one lung. The likelihood of successful surgery or treatment was remote because the cancer was already at an advanced stage. The advice was to take her home to Birmingham and speak with their doctors there.

Still in a state of silent shock, Les Cygne Four continued their rigid routine of rehearsals and performances, with mechanical precision and skill. Dora demanded that they did so. 'I've had doctors talking about me and telling us all what's to be done or rather what *can't* be done, but we *will* finish this tour. I won't let you down. You know I can do it.'

True to form Dora battled on, giving her best with each performance, thrilling and delighting her audiences, surviving on the natural rush of adrenaline that was inspired by the opening bars of their music, the thrill of each curtain rise and sheer willpower. When the final show was over and the audience clapped Dora for the very last time, her face was radiant with joy and achievement and as they entered the dressing room she threw herself into Jack's arms. 'I love you, I love our life in the theatre, but now I'm ready to go home to Birmingham.'

The next day, travelling home in the Packard, Dora was exhausted. Her head rested on Ida's shoulder and she slept. Halfway home they all enjoyed a picnic and flasks of tea and found themselves laughing and joking as if everything was normal again as they sat on a checked blanket amidst rolling hills. Louis suddenly felt guilty, but when he saw how relaxed and happy Dora was, he realised that they needed to laugh. They needed to fill Dora's remaining time with many moments of laughter and love.

When they were safely home in Birmingham, Annie arranged for her new National Health Service doctor to see Dora. She had every confidence in the NHS and was pleased when Dora was also referred to an NHS specialist. Sadly, the diagnosis remained the same. The cancer was advanced and Dora may have just months left to live.

'There must be something that can be done,' demanded Jack, as the specialist explained the kind of care Dora would need to help her deal with the pain and exhaustion as it increased.

'Let's pay for the very best medical expert available,' begged Louis.

'The diagnosis and recommendations will be the same,' explained the middle-aged specialist calmly, shaking his head in sympathy. 'You paid for private doctors before you brought her home. Things will not change.'

Despite her own emotional pain and fear of facing the loss of another child, Annie remained a tower of strength and support for everyone. One evening, having settled Dora upstairs for an early night, she summoned them all to the living room. 'Our Dora's spoken with me and she understands everything she's to face, but...' Annie paused suddenly, at the thought of what lay ahead. Gathering strength she continued, 'Dora's adamant the three of you must carry on with the act, while Hilda and I nurse her here. She'll have the best care and Madeleine will help at the weekends. She'll not have you staying and working in Birmingham. She wants the act to go on. I'm the one telling you, because she's not strong enough for any of your arguments.'

'She's my wife, I'll not leave her,' Jack covered his face with his hands, his voice rising with emotion. 'Dear Lord, why must this happen?'

Annie placed a steadying hand on Jack's shoulder. 'You have my promise, I'll not let her pass away from this world without having you beside her. Now you must be strong for her sake.'

The next morning Jack and Dora emerged from their bedsitting room extremely early, wrapped up warm and walked in the back garden together. Eventually they sat on a small bench, beside a beautifully tended flower garden and rockery. Dora drew Jack close to her and kissed him on his lips. 'I love you always, in this life and the next. Now, Jack, today we start to plan your three-handed act. Please don't argue.'

'But you know Louis and I can easily get office work in Birmingham and…'

'And waste everything we've all worked so hard for?' asked Dora with an edge to her voice. 'I'll not have any of you do that, but I promise that when I know I need you all beside me, I'll ask our mama to tell you to come home.'

Later that day, Les Cygne Four gathered in Jack and Dora's bedsitting room and under her gentle guidance, Jack, Ida and Louis were encouraged to plan their new routine.

'What will we call it?' asked Louis.

'Les Cygnes is simple and people will still know who we are,' responded Jack.

'If the agent wants to change it, then you could say Trio Cygne,' suggested Dora.

'Trio Cygne, that has a good ring to it if a change is needed,' agreed Ida.

The following week, Jack, Ida and Louis left Birmingham to sign a new contract and begin a new tour.

Away from the rigorous routine of travel, rehearsals and performances, Dora seemed to gain a little strength and energy again. In June of 1953 she helped some local ladies to raise money for a street party to celebrate the Queen's Coronation and throughout the summer she started to create several little pieces of embroidery for family members. She even walked to Handsworth Park with Hilda and Madeleine and enjoyed family evenings around the piano.

In the middle of September Jack, Ida and Louis arrived back in Birmingham, causing Annie rather a shock. 'Whatever will our Dora say?'

'She knows,' responded Jack. 'I told her when I spoke with her on the phone, last week. She said it would be a good surprise for everyone.'

'Wasn't she annoyed?'

'No, she understood, because well... we're deliberately *just resting* until January – through choice. Our show finished yesterday. We've a promise of a really good long revue from January and we deserve a break. We need to see Dora. Where is she?'

'Asleep on top of her bed. *Just resting,*' replied Annie with a smile.

Jack crept up the stairs, into their bedsitting room and gently planted a kiss on Dora's forehead. Her eyes flickered, she looked up at him, smiled and drew him onto the bed beside her. The two lay silently in each other's arms, until they were disturbed by Louis and Ida.

Finally, Les Cygne Four were together again, for a little while, enjoying each other's company. Often, in the afternoon, after a gentle walk to the park – or if Dora was tired, a short drive – they would retire to Jack and Dora's large bedsitting room and sit in armchairs around the glowing coal fire, floral tiled fireplace and pretty white mantelpiece with its picture of Joan and her family in America and various little antiques that Jack and Dora had collected on their recent tours. They would sit simply chatting and reminiscing about old times – especially childhood. Jack was happy, quietly listening to Ida, Louis and Dora's tales, knowing Dora was reliving treasured memories.

'Whatever happened to the old family field?' asked Ida suddenly, one Saturday. 'Did Pa and Uncle Edward really own it?'

'I don't know,' replied Dora, 'but when Hilda and I were just tots, Pa used to say his grandfather had owned more land years ago and that was the only bit left.'

'He told me that too,' agreed Louis. 'I used to like catching the train there every summer.'

'We had some fun, didn't we?' reminisced Dora. 'Camping in those old wooden huts, with Mama, Pa, Uncle Edward and all the cousins. All those blackberry bushes, trees to climb, wildflowers and rabbits. Two weeks every year. It was like, like paradise.'

'Our Uncle Edward taught me my times table in that blackberry field,' reminisced Louis. 'He made me keep reciting it as we picked blackberries. Seemed easier than at school somehow and he gave me a whole plate of blackberries afterwards.'

'It was Hilda and I who ended up washing all the clothes you little ones covered in blackberry stains,' laughed Dora.

'You never did like school much, did you, our Louis?' teased Ida.

'I was always being told I'd never be as clever as our brother Harold,' responded Louis. 'He was very clever. I still remember him, though he died when I was five, but it seemed wrong somehow, to keep on at me that way.'

'Tell us about the time your English master pulled you up for not paying attention,' begged Dora.

'You know it already,' protested Louis.

'Yes, but I like hearing it.'

'Well,' started Louis, 'you know I've always loved

Shakespeare and recited his plays at home sometimes. It was the last week of school. I was fourteen and daydreaming a bit, looking through the window. Suddenly the master banged his fist on my desk, *"Recite Julius Caesar, act three, scene one, NOW."* He thought I'd not know it, but of course it's an easy speech and I knew it. I acted it with all the right intonations and he stood there shocked. He went red in the face and shouted, *"Where have you been hiding yourself, you foolish boy? You should have been starring in all the school plays".*

'And so you should have been,' responded Dora laughing.

Sometimes Les Cygnes Four were joined in the bedsitting room by Madeleine, Hilda and even their mother, as if setting the pace for a time when Dora would be unable to walk, but still able to enjoy the presence of her family. Swiftly, as the last of the warmth slipped away and the colder autumn weather swept in, Dora seemed to slip a little further away from them. There were often days when she was too exhausted to come downstairs, her digestion was troubling her and she was frequently breathless and in much pain. In November she was suddenly anxious to complete all the embroidery she was doing for family members and worked for a little while each day until she finished it all. Ultimately, Jack and Dora's bedsitting room became the hub of the house – the whole family sitting up there with armchairs and footstools around the bed. They would share news with Dora, sing her favourite songs upon request and slip quietly from the room when she needed to sleep. Dora died on the 19th of November 1953, at eleven-thirty p.m.

CHAPTER 31
CINDERELLA

As Les Cygnes continued their tours – maintaining their loyalty and passion for the theatre, Louis and Vera continued to write and meet up as often as they could. Despite touring in separate shows, frequently at different ends of the country, they had fallen deeply in love and one afternoon, whilst Vera was on tour in her home county of Surrey, staying at her parents' home and Les Cygnes were in London, they snatched time to meet in Trafalgar Square. Vera was planning to take Louis by train to meet her parents for Louis had rehearsed a speech – asking for her hand in marriage. As the train rattled along, the words of his speech rattled too, vibrating within his head.

'This is our stop,' called Vera suddenly.

Louis felt proud to be walking beside Vera as she led the way through the streets to an extremely long leafy avenue of 1930s houses. She looked beautiful in her pretty floral outfit, with its slender waistline and full skirt, swinging as she walked.

'This is the one.' She reached for the gate and taking Louis' hand, led him past a fairly long front lawn, edged with flowers, towards the front door. 'I've a key, but Mother will be in and so will Dad.'

'Is this the house you said you were born in?'

'No, that's the one in Guildford. Dad still owns it. He rents it out.' She placed her key in the lock and opened the front door.

'Is that my little Vera,' came a friendly female voice from somewhere deep within the house. Instantly a door burst open and a smartly dressed, grey-haired lady in her late-fifties bustled towards Vera and wrapped her within her arms. 'And I do believe you must be Louis, I've heard a great deal about you. I was so sorry to hear about your poor sister.'

'Ah I missed you coming in. So sorry, my dear, I just popped out to water the garden,' greeted a slim almost bald gentleman, also in his late-fifties. He gave Vera a swift embrace and a quick kiss on the cheek, then offered Louis his hand. 'It's good to finally meet you. I'm Griff. Let's go into the lounge. Would you like a drink – sherry, whisky or something else perhaps?'

'Tea would be lovely if it's not too much trouble.'

'Connie dear, would you mind?' Griff looked across at his wife.

'I'll come with you, Mum,' said Vera exiting the room and hoping Louis would plunge in and ask the all-important question, whilst she and her mother were in the kitchen.

Seated within the comfortable lounge with its open piano and a violin beside it, Louis felt a little more relaxed. A large tabby cat walked into the room, wove its way around Louis' legs then jumped onto the piano stool and curled up.

'Griff,' ventured Louis, 'I've only just met you, but I've something important to ask of you.'

Griff looked up, years of wisdom present within his eyes. 'I think, perhaps, I should ask the ladies to drink their tea in the dining room?'

'Perhaps,' agreed Louis.

Griff hurried along to the kitchen. 'Connie… I'll take the tea for Louis and me. We're going to have a little chat together presently. You ladies take yours to the dining room or the garden may still be warm enough. It was quite pleasant out there a little while ago.'

Hurrying back to the lounge and firmly closing the door behind him, Griff sat opposite Louis, passed him his tea and waited.

Feeling reasonably confident Louis rushed into his speech once more. 'I've known your daughter for two years now and we've grown to love one another. I've discovered true love through knowing Vera and I would like to ask for your permission to marry her one day.'

Griff looked directly into Louis' eyes. 'Ah, but what is *true* love? What does it *really* mean to you?'

'It's... it's hard to define how I feel,' faltered Louis, 'but... but for me true love is a genuine admiration and a deep, lasting affection between two people who want to be together forever. That's the way I feel about Vera. I want to be with her always and I want to work hard to make her life happy eternally.'

'How will you support her and keep her safe? What are your plans, both of you?'

'We'd like to be engaged and continue as we are, working in the theatre, Vera singing solo and building her career and me carrying on with Les Cygnes, but in a few years we'd like to marry, settle down and perhaps leave the theatre. I'm a skilled cabinet maker, I've a business qualification from night school and I'm happy to do any honest work.'

'Well, I can see you're in earnest and I believe you care for my daughter very deeply. She doesn't need my permission to marry, but I respect the fact that you've asked. I think we should speak about this again, but for the moment I'd like to wait before I give you both my blessing.'

'Oh... yes. I think I understand,' responded Louis,

knowing Griff was aware of the age difference between he and Vera and feeling as though his very being would explode with disappointment.

Meanwhile, whilst sitting in the dining room with her mother, Vera had shared her hopes and dreams of marriage, but instead of her parents embracing the idea, Louis had returned to London feeling extremely down and Vera begged her father to explain why he had not given his blessing straight away.

'I'm sorry, my dear,' exclaimed Griff, 'he's a fine person, but there's a biggish age difference between you. As he ages, you will be nursing him. Have you considered that?'

'Yes, but I don't care. I love him with all my heart. We're kindred spirits intertwined in our love for life, music, art, literature, travel, theatre – I've never found anyone like him, he's…'

'What about your plans to go to Canada and visit your mother's sister over there? Does Louis know about that idea and how much it means to you?'

'Yes, but we'll both save up and visit one day.'

'Now here's an idea for you to consider,' offered Griff. 'Take some time, think about it and let me know. I'll pay for you to go to Canada for six months' holiday with your auntie and after that six months, if you still feel the same way about Louis, you shall have my blessing, both of you.'

Vera's answer was instant. 'No, I choose Louis over Canada. I choose playing Cinders and sharing time with Louis over Canada.'

'Cinders?' questioned Griff, somewhat puzzled.

'I'm playing principal girl – *Cinderella*, in pantomime in Weymouth this year. Louis is playing a theatre in

London, but he's driving down late on Christmas Eve and staying in digs near me for one night – though he probably won't arrive at the digs until about three in the morning – just so that we can have Christmas Day together. I couldn't get him into my digs. They were full. What do you think of Louis, Mum? You like him, don't you?'

'I think he genuinely loves you,' remarked her mother, 'and he would make a wonderful son-in-law, but you must consider the idea of visiting Canada. You could go, have a wonderful time, see all the places I knew as a child and then you could still come back and marry Louis.'

Whilst staying with her parents, Vera remained adamant that she did not want a free holiday in Canada. She did not need time to think. She knew she loved Louis. Ultimately, by the end of her week playing a theatre in Surrey, Louis was invited to visit between rehearsals and shows. Griff spoke with him and with Vera, in the lounge once more. 'You have my blessing, both of you. Louis, I will be proud to call you my son-in-law.'

'And so will I,' contributed Vera's mother, giving him a kiss on the cheek. Later that year, in December, Vera was playing *Cinderella* in Weymouth and as promised Louis drove many miles to spend Christmas Day with her. Vera had begged her rather mean, miserable landlady to allow Louis to join the guests for Christmas dinner. Having paid extra for his meal she had expected him to be served a full plate, instead of dried, overcooked turkey and disgusting vegetables left over from the day before, but they didn't care, they were together and they were in love.

That evening, before Louis drove back to London, they walked along the street together holding hands, happily planning their future as the wind blew fiercely, tugging at their clothing and their hair.

'I've a Christmas gift for you,' said Louis suddenly, 'will your landlady let me inside again for a while? It's too windy to unwrap things out here.'

'I've a gift for you too,' said Vera. 'I think the landlady's gone to visit her sister. She said she was going to. Let's go in.'

Quickly they entered the digs and sat together in the cold living room. Louis handed Vera a small rectangular parcel, tied in ribbon. 'Guess what's inside – look, read my message.'

'Oh, I'll have a go, but I'm not very good at guessing...' Carefully Vera read the message. It said: *All my love to the end of time.*

'Those are beautiful words, Louis. I think I...'

'You've guessed, haven't you?' replied Louis, 'I hope you like it.'

Gently Vera undid the ribbon and removed the paper. Inside was a rectangular box containing a stylish gold ladies watch, with a delicate reddish brown leather strap. 'It's beautiful,' gasped Vera, 'you shouldn't have.'

'I meant the words. I didn't just write them because of the watch.'

'I'll keep it forever and I'll never forget,' said Vera, her eyes filling with sudden tears of happiness as she and Louis stood and embraced. And Vera did keep the watch forever. She wore it throughout her theatre years, it was on her wrist when she married Louis and while their daughter was young. Many years later, when finally the watch stopped working, she wrapped it carefully and placed it in a little tin, beside a watch that she had once given to Louis.

Vera and Louis in Meon, in Hampshire.
Taken by a family member in the 1950s.

CHAPTER 32
TELEVISION OR TOP TOUR?

For over a year, since Dora's death, Les Cygnes had thrown themselves back into their hectic theatrical lifestyle, touring, rehearsing, performing, planning new moves and generally keeping busy every second of the day, deliberately denying themselves the time to grieve their loss. Somehow it had all seemed so much easier working away, whilst knowing Dora was being cared for at home. For, whilst in reality they knew her disease was terminal, there was always the secret hope of a sudden, miraculous cure – the feeling that her vibrant spirit could still return to them. Now the dull certainty of her permanent absence was overwhelming.

One day, whilst travelling up north, towards Yorkshire, they pulled over for a quiet picnic amidst the hills. The weather was a little windy, but actually quite warm and pleasant.

'Our Dora would have loved this spot,' remarked Ida. 'Look at the beautiful lake, down there,' she pointed towards the foot of the hill.

'Let's dance,' said Louis, suddenly. 'Let's dance for our Dora.'

They returned to the Packard, rummaged in the costume skip, removed their lightweight coats and outer clothing and changed into costumes. The three of them held hands as they walked back towards their picnic area and performed their adagio act on the warm and windy hillside. They danced fiercely, passionately and beautifully. Finally, joining hands again they raised their arms and faces towards the sky. 'For you, Dora,' said Jack, the tears streaming down his face.

Climbing back into the Packard their mood lightened and for the first time in many, many months they felt at peace with the world, ready to face anything.

Once settled in their digs Louis wrote his usual romantic weekly letter to Vera. Whilst Les Cygnes were up north, Vera was on tour in London, singing solo and enjoying every minute of it. When she wasn't rehearsing or performing, she would go for long walks, write poetry and sometimes put some of her writing to music.

Placing his completed letter carefully in a stamped, addressed envelope, Louis reached for his coat. 'I'm off to find a postbox.'

'Leave it with the landlady. She'll post it tomorrow,' suggested Ida.

'You know I'll not do that,' responded Louis. 'I'll not be long.'

Upon Louis' return they started planning some interesting new moves for their latest project – The Ritz Three – a comical act in full evening costume, involving a tyrannical female dancer and her two unfortunate male dancing partners. This was an idea they had created and worked upon, in addition to their normal adagio work, whilst Dora was ill.

At the time it had been a way of channelling their worried thoughts into something productive, some humour to relieve the tension, but certainly it had also proved a good way of generating more income, for to their delight a unicyclist left the show unexpectedly and The Ritz Three were welcomed aboard. The act had proved popular with audiences and was now part of their current contract, in addition to their usual serious adagio act.

'Could we include some speech?' wondered Ida. 'Or

would it distract the audience from our movements?'

'It might work,' agreed Louis, somewhat apprehensively.

Jack snatched up his pencil and scribbled frantically on his art pad for a few moments. 'How about this for an idea?' He showed them a series of sketches with some new moves and a series of suggested lines to say with each one.

'Let's try it tomorrow,' said Ida eagerly.

'We'll need to run through it first,' replied Louis, 'timing has to be precise. Can't run over the eight minutes.'

'Louis is right,' agreed Jack. 'Let's do extra rehearsals and include it next week.'

Jack's suggestion worked well and the audience roared with laughter throughout the comical dance act.

After the show a smartly dressed, tall, heavy-looking gentleman, possibly in his mid-forties, knocked persistently on their dressing room door.

'I'll not answer that until our Ida's changed,' responded Louis.

The knocking persisted.

Ida emerged from behind a screen. 'For goodness' sake answer that door, our Louis, before whoever it is makes a hole in it. I'm decent now.'

As Louis walked towards the door the knocking stopped abruptly. He opened the door just as the tall, wide gentleman was marching away.

'Did you need us?' called Louis.

'I don't *need* you, but you certainly *need* me.' He marched back towards the dressing room, entered, sat down upon an old wooden trunk and lit a cigar.

'Sorry, no smoking in our dressing room,' responded

Ida.

'Wait for me to tell you why I'm here, before you hurry me away with the threat of no smoking.'

'We'll not hear what you have to say, until you extinguish your cigar. I'll not risk all our costumes going up in flames,' replied Ida ferociously, stretching to her full five-foot height and facing him with her hands on her hips.

Hearing Ida's firm tone and observing her fierce expression, the man obediently extinguished his cigar. 'I'm here to offer you the chance of a lifetime. New for you – a chance to perform on television. To be seen by millions.'

Jack stepped forward, 'The Ritz Three? Or Les Cygnes?'

'I've no interest in The Ritz Three,' the man sounded impatient. 'Comedy is all very well, but I want drama, fear, risk, danger. In a word – adagio.'

Louis stepped forward, 'Who are you? Who do you represent? I'm Louis Cygne and this is…'

'I don't care which Cygne you are. I'm offering *Les Cygnes* a big chance,' replied the man pompously.

'That's grand,' responded Jack. 'Here's our agent's card. I'd ask you to speak with him.'

'But…'

'Thank you. Please communicate through our agent.' Jack ushered the man briskly through the door and closed it firmly.

'Well, we won't be hearing from *him* again in a hurry,' laughed Louis.

'I should think not. Not after the way he spoke to you,' replied Ida.

'My dears, my darlings, we may have just turned

down a grand opportunity,' said Jack spreading out his arms in a melodramatic manner. 'Or… we may just have had the biggest escape of our lives. *"I'm here to offer you the chance of a lifetime".'* He imitated the man's voice to perfection. Quickly grasping his sketchpad and pencil he produced an excellent, if rather cruel, likeness.

Three weeks later, when they were playing Chatham Empire, their agent informed them that they had indeed been offered the opportunity to appear in a television variety show and a follow up interview, with a further possible show, but it would interfere with their current long tour of top theatres and in his opinion if they were seen by thousands of people at once, every time they appeared on television the viewers would expect a higher level of danger.

'Well, I'll not be a part of something that's killing our theatres,' remarked Louis, after they'd spoken with their agent.

'My darlings, my dears, television screens will take over the world one day,' exclaimed Jack dramatically.

The Ritz Three –
comedy dance act.
Reproduced with the
permission of the
Library of Birmingham.
From the
Ernest Dyche Collection

The Ritz Three – comedy dance act.
Reproduced with the permission of the
Library of Birmingham.
From the Ernest Dyche Collection

CHAPTER 33
A BRAVE DECISION

In 1955, although Les Cygnes were kept busy, performing in top variety theatres throughout Britain, audiences were noticeably thinner on the ground and variety was struggling to survive. A number of good acts, known to Louis, Ida and Jack, had either left show business completely or gone over to television, a few were happy and successful, but a number of them spent their time begging for parts as extras, rather than sever all show business links completely. Others they knew were performing in second-rate theatres and spending much time just resting between tours.

Louis suddenly started to feel that Les Cygnes' days playing top theatres may be numbered. As each tour drew near to an end, the familiar mix of unease and excitement that occurred before a new tour transpired, became an ongoing fierce foreboding. He worried that it was only a matter of time before their luck ran out. People's tastes and lifestyles were changing, televisions were more accessible than a few years back and everyone seemed to be able to enjoy entertainment from their own armchair. Even Hilda, Madeleine and his mother now had a television.

Heading back to their digs by car after a lively and satisfying show with an excellent audience response, but nevertheless quite a number of empty seats, Louis attempted to voice his fears.

'Did you see the empty seats?'

'I *heard* the audience, they were wild. It went down well as always,' replied Ida.

'Are you trying to kill us all? Slow down,' demanded Jack, as Louis took advantage of a clear stretch of city road.

'I'll not slow down until you listen to me.'

'Just slow a bit,' suggested Ida. 'You know you can get in trouble for going too fast nowadays, especially in the city. There's more police.'

'They hide in eggcups and pounce before you know it,' added Jack.

'You do say some odd things sometimes,' laughed Ida, glancing at Jack. 'As for you, our Louis, I say we discuss this back at the digs, over a cup of tea.'

Louis nodded somewhat annoyed, slowing the car as he noticed some pedestrians crossing the road in a hugely haphazard fashion – rather the worst for wear, after exiting a bar.

'Is this car breaking down?' began Jack, as he felt the car lose a little speed.

'Would you like to drive?' growled Louis. 'I've never heard you offer. In fact, I...'

'Louis, whatever is wrong with you, having a go at poor Jack?' asked Ida. 'Just get us safely back, we'll see what Mrs D.'s left us for supper and we'll all have a nice cup of tea.'

Back at the digs Louis remained silent until they'd eaten supper. Taking their tea up to Louis and Jack's room, they all settled on the edge of Jack's bed.

'Now, our Louis, tell us what's making you so vexed,' said Ida.

'Oh, are you sure you want to hear me now?' Louis responded, caught between anger and sarcasm.

Jack stood up and placed his hand on Louis' shoulder. 'Yes, if it's important to you, then it's very important to all of us. Tell us what's been making you anxious lately. You've been…'

Not quite knowing where to start, Louis rushed in. 'We all know variety theatre's dying. Well, I'll not stay in and wait to become a washed up *has been*, in a world where television's in control.'

'But…' started Ida.

'They'll be no variety theatres left soon,' continued Louis.

'Variety theatres have been slowly dying for years, my dears. Demands are changing,' remarked Jack. 'Darlings, the world's changing, it's inevitable, it's what it does. Variety will evolve and reinvent itself, perhaps in some lesser form, but our days as a speciality act are numbered. Louis is voicing the inevitable.' Jack sank down, back onto the bed, head in hands.

'We've all a while yet before we've to worry about being washed up,' retorted Ida. 'Where's your spirit, you men? We're still playing good theatres.'

'Ida, you know I'm right,' said Louis. 'Think of all the acts who've been forced to leave the business or beg for crumbs in second rate shows.'

'You want to leave show business, is that it? You want to give up?' Ida faced Louis, signs of worry and fear upon her face.

'Not right now,' remarked Louis, but at the end of this tour. Let's leave while we're still at the top. Leave on a high note. We owe it to our Dora.'

'There's promise of another grand tour, after this one,' remarked Jack. 'I'm with you, Louis, if you're happy to leave after the next tour.'

Shocked at Jack's almost submissive response, realisation suddenly dawned on Ida as she observed his tired face. Jack was now in his mid-fifties, still leading the life of someone in their twenties or thirties. It wasn't just the decline of live variety that was against them, it was age too.

'Agreed,' responded Ida suddenly.

Both men looked at Ida in bewilderment. 'You mean it?' asked Louis.

'I'm forty-six. Do you think I want to be thrown around for the rest of my life? No – there's a big world out there. Plenty more to do.' Ida's voice was firm and determined as she turned briskly away, refusing to reveal the tears in her eyes.

CHAPTER 34
FINAL SHOW... FINAL WORDS

Les Cygnes lived their last months on tour in a fierce frenzy of activity, a passionate pursuit of perfection at all costs. Whilst this had always been a part of their ethos, it now became a wild craving, an almost unquenchable thirst – magnified by the need to reach that ultimate point of perfection before the audiences clapped their final applause and the curtains fell for the last time.

Silently they said their special goodbyes to many of the old familiar theatres and whilst staying with several of their favourite landladies they left little surprise gifts as tokens of appreciation, simple gifts – fancy soaps, some chocolates or perfume. For those rather unsavoury, miserable landladies, in miserable digs, they left nothing other than the usual appropriate comment in the visitors' book. Then, as they toured up north for the last time and reached familiar comfortable digs, run by Mrs Q., a happy and hospitable lady in her late fifties – previously in show business as a violinist – they were struck by the sudden change to her character. She smiled her usual smile of welcome, but it didn't quite reach her eyes. It was little over a year since they'd last seen her, but she looked much older.

As they entered the dining room – where meals were normally served – it became obvious it was in a state of recovery from fire. Some walls still had blackened, peeling wallpaper, others sported fresh paint.

'My dear, when did it happen?' asked Jack.

'Some weeks ago now,' responded Mrs Q. 'Don't you worry, your rooms have been repapered and there's no smell up there. I'm painting the kitchen and dining room last. Your meals will be in the old parlour. I've a table in there now.'

'How did it happen?' asked Ida. 'Do you know?'

'Silly old accordionist, no talent left – all washed up, but still playing whenever he gets the work. Had to chase him for his money I did. I'm sure it was him, always falling asleep in *my* armchair with a cigarette in his mouth he was.'

'Is there anything we can do?' asked Louis.

'Bless you, darlings, no. Everyone's been asking. I've survived worse.'

As the week progressed Les Cygnes noticed something else about Mrs Q. She no longer played her violin. Having previously been in show business she was used to a life of late evenings and late breakfasts and had fallen into the habit of playing for her guests as they ate their food – not that all the guests particularly enjoyed her playing, but always it was part of her routine. Suddenly the violin was silent. In fact, it was nowhere to be seen. Tentatively Ida broached the subject late one evening after supper.

'I haven't heard you play your beautiful music this week, Mrs Q.'

'It's gone, burnt with my pictures, my armchairs, the walls, the rest of it. I wouldn't mind the rest, but Violet was my life. Without music my life seems...' Mrs Q. paused. 'Anyway, that's enough of that. How did the show go?'

'Violet was the violin?'

She nodded. 'I'll never afford another, not for a long time. Got to make the house look good again for guests.'

When Les Cygnes left Mrs Q.'s at the end of the

week, they didn't leave her soap, chocolates, or perfume, but after taking their trunks to the Packard, Jack reached onto the back seat and carefully removed a rather worn, but nevertheless rather beautiful violin. Hiding it behind his back, he crept surreptitiously into the kitchen to present it to Mrs Q. Louis and Ida followed.

Tears rolled down her cheeks. 'You can't do that for me. The cost. I'll never repay you.'

'My dear, my darling, your music has given us many hours of pleasure, as it did your audiences years ago,' responded Jack. 'It's old, a bit battered and there's no case, but the strings are new. We bought it for next to nothing; really, we did. You can get yourself a better one, when you're back on your feet again.'

'This is our last tour. You must let us do something worthwhile for you. Your future guests will be lost without your violin playing,' contributed Louis.

Upon hearing Louis' words, Mrs Q. accepted the gift with a glowing smile and a promise to play for all her future guests every suppertime.

All too soon it was time for Les Cygnes' very last performance. Louis, Ida and Jack rehearsed with outstanding determination, pushing themselves to the very limit. Ironically everything that could go wrong, went wrong on that very last rehearsal, but true to tradition – the bad rehearsal led to an absolutely beautiful, breathtaking performance with the audience on the edge of their seats as Ida flew dangerously through the air and landed safely in Louis' arms, only to be swung round and round, like a skipping rope, by Louis and Jack and finally tossed through the air once more – at a fierce speed – for Louis to run and catch. As they drew together for their final pose and then joined hands swiftly bowing together, the audience clapped wildly and stood to acknowledge their praise.

Les Cygnes almost floated towards their dressing room, their bodies still full of adrenaline and awash with happiness and the knowledge that they had given their best years to the theatre.

'You boys go ahead,' said Ida, as they were about to walk past one of the dressing rooms. 'I promised I'd say goodbye to the singing duet, won't be long.' Quickly she knocked on their door, chatted for a short while and then made her way to Les Cygnes' dressing room.

'Whatever are you writing? It looks as though your very life depends upon it. What is it?' asked Ida, as she entered the dressing room and observed Louis and Jack sitting silently side by side at the wide dressing room mirror. Apparently deep in thought, Jack was hurriedly scribbling words upon a spare scrap of lined notepaper, whilst Louis was busy, staring in the mirror as he removed the greasepaint from his face.

'Just words, mere words,' Jack almost whispered his reply. 'My thoughts…' his voice trembled as he paused suddenly.

'What is it, Jack?' asked Louis, standing up and placing a firm, comforting hand on Jack's shoulder. 'Are you writing about Dora?'

'Not just Dora, all of this…' Still holding his pen, in one hand, Jack stood up, opening wide his arms to draw attention to the dressing room with its random selection of chairs, mirrors, lights, costumes and make-up, intertwined with everyday clothing. Gathering strength to his voice once more and with a glimmer of the usual wild humour returning to his eyes, he thrust the paper towards Louis. 'Here, Louis, put on your best voice, read

"*Departure*" it's dedicated to our final curtain call. Mere garbage, my dears, mere garbage, but it's *my* garbage so read it well!'

Swiftly accepting the tatty scrap of paper, Louis drew himself to his full five-foot-four, struck a theatrical pose and read Jack's words in his finest speaking voice, perfect with its gentle hint of Birmingham still present:

'*This wild, ecstatic gleam within my eye is springing forth from a soul, possessed with desire, desire to live forever within the lights and the pulsating orchestra of show business, for then I may never die, but live instead within the colour, movement and laughter eternally. The curtain may close upon our act, but never, never upon our spirits, for they were claimed by the world of theatre many moons ago. The act may linger but a while within the minds and memories of our audience, but our spirits will live again with each curtain rise.*

'*Someday, children created through our bodies, perhaps possessing our features, perhaps possessing fragments of our very souls, may experience the thrill and the longing to become part of this world of make believe, this world of music and dance – of tragedy and comedy – to which we truly belong. Whatever their dreams, let us hope they will find fulfilment and success as we have.*'

'Those are good words, Jack, strong words. Dora would have loved them,' responded Ida. 'But now, it's time to move on and our Dora would agree with me. Time to turn the page and live the next chapter of our lives. Who knows what may happen…'

ABOUT THE AUTHOR

The author is the daughter of Louis (one of the Les Cygne Four) and Vera (the soprano singer mentioned in section four of the book).

As an adult she ran a nursery school, lectured in colleges and taught online. She is married, has three grown up children and two lively grandchildren. She adores adventure, travel, running on the beach with her dog, music, poetry and white water rafting. In recent years, using the pen name of A.F.B. Griffey, she has written two poetry books for children and one lively rhyming story.

Recent books by Annette-Frances B. include:

Take a Look Again... A unique anthology of poems and musical lyrics, shared by five generations of her family – compiled with David King.

With all her books the author aims to donate most money from royalties to reputable cancer, Alzheimer's disease and childcare charities.

ACKNOWLEDGEMENTS:

This book is based on the lives and experiences of the family speciality adagio act Les Cygne Four/Les Cygnes (1932–1955). In show business their lives were touched and enriched by a number of famous theatricals including: Hylda Baker, Will Hay, Sir Harry Lauder, The Crazy Gang (Bud Flanagan and Chesney Allen, Jimmy Nervo and Teddy Knox, Charlie Naughton and Jimmy Gold) and Lucan and McShane.

The following people provided Les Cygne Four/Les Cygnes with the opportunity to perform within excellent, often spectacular productions and were always mentioned with respect and thanks: George and Harry Foster, Cissie Williams, Tommy Lorne and Elkan Simons, Mannie Jay and Sydney Myers, Harry Dennis and Lew and Leslie Grade.

Madame Helena Lehmiski

Originally from Poland, Madame Helena Lehmiski (1898/9–1988) was a unique individual to whom Les Cygne Four owed their theatrical expertise and tenacity. She worked them hard and helped them to achieve their dreams. Madame Lehmiski was a member of the Royal Academy of Dancing (RAD) – originally known as the Association of Operatic Dancing. From the mid-1950s she journeyed to New Zealand, Mexico, Canada, Africa and America for the RAD – as a lecturer, examiner and broadcaster. She taught and provided dancers for pantomimes at The Alexandra Theatre Birmingham for many years and was well known and well respected throughout the Midlands.

In 2023 the name Lehmiski still influences the world of theatre dance: The Lehmiski Academy of Dance, Acocks Green, Warwick Road, B27 6RG is organised by Principal Brenda Yeates – Theatre Dance examiner for the International Theatre Dance Awards (IDTA).

With thanks to Marie Cresitta – sadly no longer with us – for the kindness and encouragement she gave to Vera at the beginning of her show business career and with thanks for the warm welcome she gave Vera and her daughter whenever they visited her in Covent Garden.

With thanks to my editor Helen Baggott, for her patience and expertise and to my beta readers for their valuable and constructive comments.

Thank you to Hugh Farrer (retired writer, explorer and former secretary of the Kent Underground Research Group) for allowing me to quote his definition of love: "...*a genuine admiration and... two people who want to be together forever.*" within Louis' speech in chapter 31.

With grateful thanks to *The Stage* for granting permission to quote brief passages describing Les Cygne Four (each passage individually referenced and acknowledged).

With grateful thanks to *The Scotsman* for granting permission to quote a passage describing Les Cygne Four (appropriately acknowledged beneath the wording used).

Photographic content – with grateful thanks to the Library of Birmingham for granting permission to use five photographs from The Ernest Dyche Collection (MS 2912) (acknowledged on each relevant page).

With grateful thanks to Camera Press for granting permission to use photographs taken by Yvonne Gregory A.R.P.S. (acknowledged on each relevant page).

A big thank you to Alexander-Way B. for his brilliant cover design and artwork.

A big thank you to John O'Shea for providing the picture of the moon.

The wonderful font on the front cover is called Prodelt Co and was created by Graptail Type Studio. A big thank you to them for giving permission to use it.

With grateful thanks to family members for allowing me to reproduce photographs they have taken.

GENERAL NOTES

Whilst the act was usually known as *Les Cygne Four*, throughout the years they were sometimes known, billed and booked as *Maxellos*, though there was another acrobatic act, with a similar name, hence Les Cygne Four was generally used. During Dora's illness and following her death from breast cancer in 1953, the act adapted many of its dance routines and at one point they created two acts, one with comedy acrobatic dance: *The Ritz Three* and one with normal acrobatic adagio: *Trio Cygne* or simply Les Cygnes (occasionally called the Goya Trio). For the sake of simplicity, throughout each chapter I have referred to them as Les Cygne Four or Les Cygnes. Theatrical programmes and online newspaper archives offer a clearer picture regarding when and where the act used each name. As Les Cygne Four did not provide information on the interior of their dance school/s, my description is based on various dance schools within that era.

'The Waltz' from *Faust*, by Charles Gounod – used by Les Cygne Four, as backing for their act, generally lasts about four minutes, but was possibly adapted slightly or played twice – thus covering the time needed for an eight-minute act. Throughout the years their music may have changed, but this piece was the one they frequently mentioned.

Adagio Dancing was and still is a form of dance involving grace, precision, balance and counterbalance, excellent timing and exciting movements such as lifting, throwing, catching, spinning a dancer by holding his/her wrists and ankles or forming a human skipping rope. Ideally, performers are well versed in traditional ballet and all forms of theatre dance.

Examples of adagio movements are sometimes apparent within some of the exciting dance routines in shows such as *Strictly Come Dancing* and *Dancing on Ice*.

Digs – a term used by some people to describe accommodation or lodgings. Theatricals tend to use this term.

Variety – variety artistes performed their routine as part of a big variety show.

Revue – as well as their normal act, variety artistes were required to take part in various sketches and large exotic scenes, often with spectacular scenery and props, based around a specific theme, whilst working – hopefully – as part of a close-knit team.

Printed in Great Britain
by Amazon

24366451R00128